WITTS RECREATIONS

Witts Recreations

*Selected from
the finest Fancies
of Moderne Muses*

1640

A facsimile edition
with introduction
and indexes
by
Colin Gibson

Scolar Press

Published by
SCOLAR PRESS
Gower House
Croft Road
Aldershot
Hants GU11 3HR
England

Gower Publishing Company
Old Post Road
Brookfield
Vermont 05036
USA

Printed in Great Britain by
The Ipswich Book Company Ltd

British Library Cataloguing in Publication Data
Witts recreations: selected from the finest fancies of moderne
    muses 1640: a facsimile edition. – (English verse
    miscellanies of the 17th century)
    1. Poetry in English 1625–1702.
    I. Series
    821.408

    ISBN 0–85967–783–4

Contents

English Verse Miscellanies of the Seventeenth Century

Foreword by the General Editor

This series of facsimile editions is designed to make available texts of seventeenth-century English poetry that was commonly circulated in miscellanies, both manuscript and printed. The collections represented include familiar poems by many of the most celebrated names of the period, as well as much verse that is otherwise obscure or anonymous.

Limitations of format preclude detailed discussion of particular poems, authorship, dating, comparative texts and other subjects appropriate to elaborate critical editions. However, some relevant information is given, purely as a guide, in the editor's introduction and indexes. In the Table of Contents, any attribution which appears in the source is cited after the title of the poem within single inverted commas; this is followed, in square brackets, by the editor's own attribution, indicating the likely or generally accepted authorship. Uncertain or doubtful attributions which are known to occur in other sources are signalled '*attrib*'. Very brief outlines of the education and careers of identified or attributed authors are given in the Index of Authors.

For convenient reference, alphabetical Indexes of Titles and First Lines are also provided: titles according to exact wording of the original (ignoring definite and indefinite articles), and also according to the first adjective, noun or pronoun (following a preposition); first lines in modernized spelling with minimum punctuation.

Peter Beal

Introduction

Between 1630 and 1655, Humphrey Blunden, the original London publisher of *Wit's Recreations*, issued a number of religious and theological works by writers including the poet Henry Vaughan and the astrologer William Lilly. During the Civil War he published many political pamphlets and was the editor of a news-sheet which became popularly known as 'Blunden's Passages'. But in his earlier years he also published at least one play and some books of secular verse and prose; *Poetical Varieties* (1637) by Thomas Jordan, Robert Davenport's comedy *A New Trick to Catch the Devil* (1638), *The Academy of Love* (1641) by John Johnson, and the first two editions (1640 and 1641) of the poetical miscellany *Wit's Recreations*.

The Publication and its Printers

Wit's Recreations was entered in the Stationers' Register under the hand of Matthew Clay for Blunden on 15 October 1639, and published by him in 1640 as *Witts Recreations. Selected from the finest Fancies of Moderne Muses, with a Thousand outlandish Proverbs*. Clay's imprimatur, dated 8 October 1639, appears on the final page of *Wit's Recreations*, and (with only the year given) at the end of some copies of *Outlandish Proverbs*. As the double title indicates, it was a composite volume, consisting of two octavo booklets, each with their own title-page and the work of two different master printers, Richard Hodgkinson (*Wit's Recreations*) and

Thomas Paine (*Outlandish Proverbs*). *Outlandish Proverbs* was entered in the Stationers' Register on 24 September 1639, to Matthew Simmons, who later issued the fourth (1650) edition of *Wit's Recreations*. But Humphrey Blunden first published the *Proverbs* in 1640 both as a separate volume and in combination with *Wit's Recreations*. It was then dropped from all succeeding editions of *Wit's Recreations*, although, reissued in 1651 by Thomas Garthwait with a new title-page, it has its own later publishing history. Blunden may have decided that he needed to piece out *Wit's Recreations* with such additional material, or add to its attractiveness by associating it with the name of the popular author of *The Temple*. That many of the poems in *Wit's Recreations* make play with proverbs and proverbial sayings might also have suggested the pairing with the Herbert collection.

Richard Hodgkinson, the printer for *Wit's Recreations*, produced a book of very uneven quality. The 504 poems on signatures A–M were probably set by two compositors; a third man set the 126 verse epitaphs on signatures Aa–Cc. His work is clearly distinguished by the use of a larger font, a longer print measure and a separate and different numerical system, as well as by its general accuracy and correctness. The presswork of the other compositors shows every sign of haste: there are a number of obvious press errors like *Chirst* for *Christ* (No. 460) or 'I'll' for 'Ill' (No. 231), some poems are left untitled, and the number sequence is disrupted by errors, omissions and repetitions.

But despite its frequently careless printing, *Wit's Recreations* was evidently a successful publication. The two issues of the first edition, one represented by the British Library copy C. 65. c. 6, the other by the Bodleian Library copy 8⁰ a, 143. Art., and differing only in that the former copy has a cancel leaf of Ee3 and prints 1010 proverbs as against 1032 in the Bodleian and other copies, were followed by a second, greatly expanded edition in 1641. Other publishers issued successive editions in 1645, 1650, 1654, 1663, 1667 (two issues) and 1683, in the course of which the title underwent several transformations and the collection was repeatedly rearranged and considerably amplified. The 1640 edition, for instance, consisted of 504 epigrams and 126 epitaphs; by 1663, retitled *Recreations for Ingenious Head-pieces, or a Pleasant Grove for their Wits to walk in*, the miscellany offered 700 epigrams, 200 epitaphs, a number of fancies and an abundance of 'fantastics', 'With their new Addition, Multiplication, and Division'.

Dedication and Authorship

Blunden dedicated his book to Francis Newport (1619–1708), then a young man of 21 and the future Earl of Bradford. Educated at Gray's Inn (1633), the Middle Temple (1634) and Christ Church, Oxford (1635), where many of the known contributors to the miscellany had themselves received an education, Newport would have been well acquainted with the tradition of witty writing and might be expected to appreciate such a dedication.

It is unlikely that Humphrey Blunden collected the poems gathered in *Wit's Recreations* himself. Although there is general agreement that the initials of the compiler of *Outlandish Proverbs*, 'G.H.', stand for the poet George Herbert, the anthologist who assembled *Wit's Recreations* has not yet been identified. As Timothy Raylor has pointed out, there is no direct evidence that Sir John Mennes or James Smith, to whom it is frequently attributed, were involved in its authorship; the common ascription to Mennes and Smith has largely arisen from the inclusion of *Wit's Recreations* with two other seventeenth-century miscellanies which do contain material by Smith and Mennes, *Musarum Deliciae* (1655) and *Wit Restored* (1658), in *Facetiae*, edited by Thomas Park and Edward Dubois in 1817. In the absence of any other obvious candidate, it seems worth suggesting the name of Thomas Jordan (1614?–1685), a prolific writer whose first verse collection, *Poetical Varieties, or Variety of Fancies*, was published by Humphrey Blunden in 1637, and who went on to produce several miscellanies with titles resembling the full

xi

title of *Wit's Recreations*: namely, *Claraphil and Clarinda, in a Forest of Fancies* (1650); *A Royal Arbor of Loyal Poesie* (1664); a collection of 'acrosticks, anagrams, epigrams, elegies and epitaphs', *A Nursery of Novelties in a Variety of Poetry* (1665?); *Wit in a Wilderness of Promiscuous Poesie* (*c.*1660) and *The Muses' Melody in a Consort of Poetry* (1680?).

As was the usual practice in miscellanies of this period the 630 epigrams, epitaphs, lyrical and anagrammatic poems that make up *Wit's Recreations* are printed without attribution. A few of the identifications proposed in the present edition derive from Margaret Crum's *First Line Index of English Poetry 1500–1800 in Manuscripts of the Bodleian Library, Oxford*, but the great majority of them are the work of the scholar George Thorn-Drury (1860–1931), who extensively annotated a copy of Hotten's 1874 edition of Park and Dubois's *Facetiae* now in the Bodleian Library (Thorn-Drury, e. 4,5).

Contents

The 630 poems in the collection span a period of nearly forty years, the earliest of them celebrating events near the turn of the century such as the deaths of Sidney (E114), Drake (146), Spenser (E70) and Sir Horatio Palavicino (62), with several poems appropriated from John Weever's *Epigrams* of 1599. The latest dateable poem (135) clearly alludes to the wounding of Colonel Goring at the siege of Breda on 6 September 1637.

There are relatively few dramatist-poets represented here, though poems by Marlowe, Shakespeare, Jonson, and Beaumont and Fletcher do appear. With such notable exceptions as Corbett, Carew, Wotton, Cowley, Browne, Strode, Quarles and Randolph, the majority of writers identifiable by name are among the many occasional versifiers, epigrammatists, translators and minor poets who came from the ranks of the wits and college men of the period, reflecting the rhetorical training they received at such schools as Westminster and later at the Universities of Oxford or Cambridge and at the Inns of Court. Oxford's importance in the first half of the seventeenth century as a centre for the production and publication of such verse is shown in the number of Oxford writers (26 of them, as against 13 Cambridge men), but *Wit's Recreations* is much more than an anthology of the work of the university wits. The compiler drew heavily on published sources – the numerous borrowings from Thomas Bastard's *Chrestoleros* (1598), John Davies' *The Scourge of Folly* (1611?), Henry Parrot's *Laquei Ridiculosi* (1613), Henry Fitzgeffrey's *Certain Elegies* (1618) and Robert Hayman's *Certain Epigrams* (1628) are cases in point – as well as collecting popular poetry circulating in private copies. Other texts of one fifth of the epigrams and half the epitaphs printed in *Wit's Recreations* exist in the manuscripts held in the Bodleian Library alone.

Although almost all of the poetry which makes up the collection might be described as word-games, *Wit's Recreations* is particularly rich in poems (119 of them) whose *raison d'être* is some witty play on a proverb or name, or which relate, often at considerable length, the occasions of quips, jests and clever retorts. Riddles are not uncommon, and punning is usual in this group. Thirty-eight poems address topics directly concerned with literature, language and books; there are poems on critics, readers, poets, rhetoricians and book-buyers, and the number might be largely extended by the inclusion of translations into English or Latin, such epigrams founded on literary conceits as 116, 'Women are books and men the readers be', and poems dealing with European as well as English writers and scholars.

Another considerable group of poems (61 of them) take as their subject historical persons, most of them the contemporaries or recent contemporaries of readers of the collection. Particularly striking is the number of literary figures, poets, translators, and dramatists, who figure in the miscellany. Ben Jonson (three poems) and Shakespeare lead the dramatists, but an unusual number of other playwrights are mentioned: Beaumont and Fletcher, Heywood, Middleton, Massinger, Ford, Goffe, Suckling and Barten Holyday. George Sandys is praised for his translation of Ovid (1621–6), Chapman for his Homer (1616), May for his Lucan (1626–7), Habington for his *Castara* (1634), and Wither for his *Abuses Stripped and Whipped* (1613), together with more general praise for Chaucer, Spenser, Drayton, Randolph, Phineas Fletcher and Thomas Tusser.

There are tributes to royal and aristocratic figures such as Queen Elizabeth, Queen Anne of Denmark, Elizabeth of Bohemia, the much mourned Prince Henry (four poems), the Protestant hero Gustavus Adolphus of Sweden (two poems), and other scandalous or heroic names – Sir Horatio Palavicino, Lady Rich, Ralegh and Sidney. But many more ordinary men and women find mention: Thomas Hobson, the University of Cambridge carrier, whose death on 1 January 1631 provoked a flurry of verses (there are six of them here), Master Carter, the victim of a gunpowder explosion at Finsbury in 1625/6, Dr Goad, the actor Burbage, and others like Susanna Horsenell, Elizabeth Noell or Christopher Lawson, known only through the poems in which they are named.

A popular topos for these versifiers (65 poems) is a trade or occupation, with the writers displaying their skill and language consciousness by playing wittily on professional jargon and technical terms. The largest number of such pieces deal with familiar city trades and country occupations, followed by poems on the legal profession, soldiers and servants, with a few poems each on doctors, performing artists, merchants, money-lenders, and the underworld of criminals and vagrants.

Another large group of poems deal with sexuality, expressed in terms of lovers and married couples, and the perennial subject of female beauty. Cynical, sentimental or bawdy, they are usually conventional in theme, trading the traditional witticisms about the follies of lovers, the inequalities of marriage, and anti-feminist jokes about female garrulousness, inconstancy and amorousness. On the other hand, the collection includes several epitaphs in which women are remembered with respect and deep affection, as well as some twenty-five lyrical love poems.

Although the prevailing tone of the poems in *Wit's Recreations* is comic and light-hearted, in such a large collection there is room for a number of poems on what in No. 105 is called 'our frail mortalitie'. The effects of time, death (particularly the death of children), fortune, human sinfulness and the comforts or discomforts of religion find expression in sober and meditative verse, as well as in more irreverent poems. Puritan zeal and Roman Catholicism are satirized in equal measure, in keeping with the latitudinarian temper of the miscellany, and such poetry is mixed indiscriminately with comic and satirical observations on a host of more worldly topics: female fashion and the ridiculous behaviour of young gallants, food, drink and the taking of tobacco, social climbing and ostentatious wealth, mockery and abuse of physical oddities, 'foreigners' (especially the Spanish, the French and the Welsh), and the civilized arts of music, painting, jewellery, cosmetics and writing itself, together with witty effusions on such set topics as a blocked pump, the weights of a clock, a pound of candles or a pair of tongs.

Collectively, a miscellany such as this not only exemplifies the range of minor poetry and occasional verse that constituted popular reading in the period; it also provides a vivid panorama of social life under the Stuarts, in which tennis court habitués, tobacconists, thieves, gamblers, sextons, lawyers, fencing masters, sailors, prostitutes, butchers, scholars, musicians, usurers, barbers, soldiers, drunkards, footmen and porters rub shoulders with Westminster officials, scriveners, farmers and country gentlemen, falconers, gardeners, alehouse-keepers, wandering beggars, cooks, cobblers, wealthy city women, quarrelling couples, tavern friends and grieving parents.

Colin Gibson

A Note on the Text

The exemplar of *Wit's Recreations* reproduced in the present facsimile edition is a copy in the British Library (pressmark C. 56. c. 6). The octavo volume is made up of five unnumbered leaves, B–L^8, M^4, Aa–Cc^8. The contents are: engraved half-title signed 'W. Marshall', verso blank; title, verso blank; verse explanation of the half-title, verso blank; dedication to 'Francis Newport, Esq.' signed 'Humphrey Blunden', verso blank; publisher's verse preface, verso blank; one hundred and sixty-five text pages; three blank pages; forty-eight text pages. Signatures D4, E4, F4, G4, H3 and L4 are unsigned; K3 and Bb2 are mis-signed R3 and Aa2.

Since the volume is unpaged, indexes in the present edition are keyed to the original sequential numbering of the poems, with the separate series of epitaphs distinguished by the prefix 'E'. Where errors occur in these sequences, the original number is followed by the correct number supplied in square brackets; duplicated numbers are distinguished as, for instance, 168 and 168 *bis*. Editorial emendation of the material in the indexes is kept to a minimum, and shown in square brackets, as 'On a W[r]estler' (E34). In the index of authors, an asterisk is used to distinguish a translation from an original poem.

Literature and References

Cambridge Bibliography of English Literature [where *Wit's Recreations* is mistakenly attributed to Sir John Mennes and James Smith]

Arthur E. Case, *A Bibliography of English Poetical Miscellanies 1521–1750* (Oxford, 1935), No. 95

Margaret Crum, *First-Line Index of English Poetry 1500–1800 in Manuscripts of the Bodleian Library Oxford*, 2 vols (Oxford, 1969)

G. Blakemore Evans, 'Milton and the Hobson Poems', *Modern Language Quarterly*, 4 (1943), 281–90

———— 'A Correction to "Some More Hobson Verses"', *Modern Language Quarterly*, 9 (1948), 184

Colin A. Gibson, 'Elizabethan and Stuart Dramatists in *Wit's Recreations* (1640)', *Research Opportunities in Renaissance Drama*, 29 (1986–7), 15–23

Facetiae, ed. Thomas Park and Edward Dubois, 2 vols (London, 1817)

Facetiae, ed. J. C. Hotten, 2 vols (London, 1874)

The Works of George Herbert, ed. F. E. Hutchinson (Oxford, 1953)

R. B. McKerrow, *A Dictionary of Printers and Booksellers . . . 1557–1640*, 5 vols (London, 1907–32)

W. R. Parker, 'Milton's Hobson Poems: Some Neglected Early Texts', *Modern Language Review*, 31 (1936), 395–402

Norman Philip, '*Musarum Deliciae*, 1656', *Notes & Queries*, 11th Series, 9 (1914), 37

Robert Pierpont, '*Musarum Deliciae*, 1656', *Notes & Queries*, 11th Series, 9 (1914), 37

LITERATURE AND REFERENCES

Margaret C. Pitman, 'The Epigrams of Henry Peacham and Henry Parrot', *Modern Language Review*, 29 (1934), 129–36

Timothy Raylor, '*Wit's Recreations* not by Sir John Mennes or James Smith?', *Notes & Queries*, 230 (1985), 2–3

———— *The Achievement of Sir John Mennes and Dr James Smith*, unpublished DPhil thesis (Oxford, 1986)

David C. Redding, 'Some Epigrams attributed to Sir John Davies', *Notes & Queries*, 206 (1961), 426–7

Franklin B. Williams, 'Henry Parrot's Stolen Feathers', *Publications of the Modern Languages Association*, 52 (1937), 1019–30

Acknowledgements

I would like to thank Professor Alistair Fox, Mary Sullivan, Jane Jones and Martin Andrew for their assistance in the preparation of this edition. The Bodleian Library, Oxford, made available a microfilm of G. Thorn-Drury's annotated copy of *Facetiae* (1874), and the British Library provided photographs of the copy of the 1640 edition of *Wit's Recreations* which forms the basis of the present edition.

Table of Contents

TABLE OF CONTENTS

TABLE OF CONTENTS

TABLE OF CONTENTS

TABLE OF CONTENTS

TABLE OF CONTENTS

TABLE OF CONTENTS

TABLE OF CONTENTS

[Facsimile text of *Wit's Recreations*: Half-title (1 page); verso blank; title (1 page); verso blank; 'The Frontispeice discovered' (1 page); verso blank; Dedication to Francis Newport (1 page); verso blank; 'The Stationer to the Reader' (1 page); verso blank; text of epigrams (170 pages) + text of epitaphs (48 pages)]

The Frontespeice discovered.

This spreading Vine, like these choyce Leaves invites
The Curteous eye to tast her choyce Delights.
These painefull Bees, presented to thy view,
Shewes th'Author works not for himselfe, but you.
The windy Musick, that salutes thine eye,
Bespeakes thine Eare, thy judgement standing by.
The Devious Horseman, wandring in this Maze,
Shewes Error, and her execrable wayes :
Whose brazen Insolence, and boldnesse urges
The hornefoot Satyres to their angry Scourges :
And he that Drawes his Sword against the Swarme
Of Waspes, is he, that lasht, begins to storme.

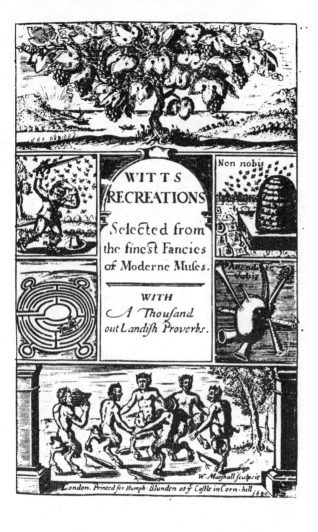

The Stationer to
the Reader.

IF *new or old wit please the reader best*,
  I've hope each man of wit will be our guest,
The new was fram'd to humor some mens taste;
Which if they like not, they may carve the last :
Each dish hath sauce belongs to't, and you will
By your dislike, censure the Authors skill;
Yet if you cannot speake well of it, spare
To utter your dislike, that the like snare
May entrap others; *so the booke may bee*
Sold, though not lik'd, by a neate fallacy :
That's all I aske yet 'twill your goodnes raise,
If as I gaine your coyn, he may your praise.

Wits Recreations.

1 *To the Reader.*

Xcuse me Reader though I now and
than
In some light lines doe shew my
selfe a man,
Nor be so sowre, some wanton
words to blame
They are the language of an Epigram.

2 On *Battus.*

Battus doth bragge he hath a world of bookes
His studies maw holds more then well it may,
But seld' or never he upon them looks
And yet he looks upon them every day,

B   He

✦✦✦✦✦✦✦✦✦✦✦✦✦✦✦✦✦✦✦✦✦✦✦✦✦✦✦✦

He looks upon their out-fide, but within
He never looks, nor never will begin :
Becaufe it cleane againft his nature goes
To know mens fecrets, fo he keeps them clofe.

3 *On the fame*

I pray thee *Battus*, adde unto thy ftore
This booke of mine to make thy number more ;
It is well bound, well printed, neatly ftrung,
And doth deferve to have a place among
Th'inhabitants of thy Vatican, if thou
Wilt fo much favor to its worth allow.

4 *An evill age.*

Virgill of *Mars* and ruthfull wars did treat,
Ovid of *Venus* love, and peace did write :
Yet *Virgill* for his ftrain was counted great,
And *Ovid* for his love was bannifhed quite ;
    No marvell then if courtezie grow cold ,
    When hate is prais'd and love it felf control'd.

5 *On a womans will.*

How dearly doth the fimple husband buy,
His wiv's defect of will, when fhe doth dy ?
                           Bet-

Better in death by will to let her give,
Then let her have her will whilst she doth live.

6 To a wise reader.

Thou say'st these verses are rude, ragged, rough,
Not like some others, rimes smooth dainty stuffe:
Epigrames are like satires rough without,
Like chesse-nuts sweet, take thou the kernell out.

7 Of a Judge.

Were I to choose a Captain I would than,
Not choose your courtier or a youthfull man,
No, I would choose a judge, one grim and grave:
To make a Captain such a man I'de crave:
Give me that man, whose frowning brow is death,
I, such an one, as can kill men with breath.

8 Of Poetus.

Poetus with fine sonnets painteth forth,
This and that foul Ladyes beauties worth:
He shewes small wit thereby, and for his paines,
By my consent he never shall reape gains,
Why what need poets paint them? O sweet Elves!
When Ladyes paint their beauties best themselves.

9 *On an up-ſtart.*

Pray wrong not(late-coyn'd)give the man his right
He's made a gentleman although no knight,
For now 'tis cloths the gentleman doth make,
Men from gay cloths their pedigrees do take;
But wot you what's the armes to ſuch mens houſe?
Why this——hands chacing of a rampant louſe.

10 *Ad Clodium.*

Wit,once thou ſaid'ſt was worth thyweight in gold
Though now't be common for a trifle ſold;
It dearer ſeems to thee, that get'ſt not any,
When thou ſhould'ſt uſe it, for thy love or money

11 *In Getam.*

Geta from wool and weaving firſt began,
Swelling and ſwelling to a gentleman,
When he was gentleman and bravely dight:
He left not ſwelling till he was a knight;
At laſt forgetting what he was at firſt,
He ſwole to be a Lord,and then he burſt.

12 *In Fimum.*

Fimus is coach'd and for his farther grace,
Doth aske his friends how he becomes the place;
Troth I should tell him, the poor coach hath wrong
And that a cart would serve to carry dung.

13 *Asperum nimis condimentum.*

Monsieur *Albanus* new invested is,
With sundry suits and fashions passing fit,
But never any came so neer as this,
For joy whereof *Albanus* frollique is:
    Untill the Taylours bill of *solvi sin,*
    Diverts his humor to another bias.

14 *Gender and number.*

Singular sins and plurall we commit;
And we in every gender vary it.

15 *Atheists pastimes.*

Grammarians talk of times past and hereafter:
I spend time present in pastime and laughter.

To

♦♦♦♦♦♦♦♦♦♦♦♦♦♦♦♦♦♦♦♦♦♦♦♦♦♦♦♦♦♦♦♦

EPIGRAMS.

16 *To Sr. John Suckling.*

If learning will beseem a Courtier well,
If honour waite on those who dare excell,
Then let not Poets envy but admire,
The eager flames of thy poetique fire;
For whilst the world loves wit, Aglaura shall,
Phœnix-like live after her funerall.

17 *On a braggadocio.*

Don *Lollus* brags, he comes of noble blood,
Drawn down from *Brutus* line, tis very good;
If this praise-worthy be, each flea may then,
Boast of his blood more then some gentlemen.

18 *To Mr. George Sands.*

Sweet-tongued *Ovid*, though strange tales he told,
Which gods and men did act in dayes of old,
What various shapes for love sometimes they took,
To purchase what they aym'd at; could he look,
But back upon himself he would admire,
The sumptuous bravery of that rich attire;
Which

Which *Sands* hath clad him with,& then place this
His change amongst their Metamorphosis.

19 *To Mr. William Habbington on his Castara, a Poem.*

Thy Muse is chaste and thy *Castara* too,
'Tis strange at Court, & thou hadst power to woo
An1 to obtain(what others were deny'd)
The fair *Castara* for thy vertuous bride :
　　Enjoy what you dare wish, and may there bee,
　　Fair issues branch from both, to honor thee.

20 *To Mr. Francis Beaumont and Mr. John Fletcher gent.*

Twin-stars of poetry, whom we justly may,
Call the two-tops of learn'd Pernassus-Bay,
Peerlesse for freindship and for numbers sweet ;
Whom oft the Muses swaddled in one sheet :
　　Your works shall still be prais'd and dearer sold,
　　For our new-nothings doe extoll your old.

21 *On a pump stopt with stones.*

M. I'le cut it down, I swear by this same hand,
　　If 'twill not run, it shall no longer stand.
　　　　　　B 4　　　　　*R.* Pray

✦✦✦✦✦✦✦✦✦✦✦✦✦✦✦✦✦✦✦✦✦✦✦✦✦✦✦✦

R. Pray fir be patient, let your pump alone,
　　How can it water-make when't hath the ftone.
Yet did he wifely when he did it fell,
For in fo doing he did make it well.

22 To Mr. Benjamin Johnfon.

Had Rome but heard her worthies fpeak fo high,
As thou haft taught them in thy Poefie ;
She would have fent her poets to obtain ,
(Tutour'd by thee) thy moft majeftique ftrain.

23 In Aulam.

Thou ftill art mutring *Aulus* in mine eare,
Love me and love my dog, I will I fwear,
Thou ask'ft but right and *Aulus* truth to tell,
I think thy dog deferves my love as well.

24 To Mr. George Chapman on his Tranflation of Homers works into Englifh meeter.

Thou Ghoft of *Homer* 'twere no fault to call ,
His the trnflation thine the Originall,
Did we not know 'twas done by thee fo well;
Thou makeft *Homer*, *Homers* felf excell.

❦❦❦❦❦❦❦❦❦❦❦❦❦❦❦❦❦❦❦❦❦❦❦❦

25 *To Mr. William Shake-spear.*

Shake-speare we must be silent in thy praise,
'Cause our encomion's will but blast thy Bayes,
Which envy could not, that thou didst do well;
Let thine own histories prove thy Chronicle.

26 *Ad Tilenum.*

Tilenus 'cause th' art old, fly not the field,
Where youthfull *Cupid* doth his banner weild
For why? this god, old men his souldiers stil'd
None loves, but he, who hath bin twice a child.

27 *To Mr. Thomas Randolph.*

Thou darling of the Muses for we may
Be thought deserving, if what was thy play
Our utmost labours can produce, we will
Freely allow thee heir unto the hill,
The Muses did assign thee, and think 't fit,
Thy younger yeares should have the elder-wit.

28 *In Paulum.*

Paul what my cloak doth hide thou fain wouldst
Were't to be seen I would not cover't so. (know

‡‡‡‡‡‡‡‡‡‡‡‡‡‡‡‡‡‡‡‡‡‡‡‡‡‡‡‡‡‡‡‡‡

29 *Of sleep and death.*

That death is but a sleep I not deny
Yet when I next would sleep, I would not dy.

30 *Ad Lectorem.*

Reader thou see'st how pale these papers look,
Whiles they fear thy hard censure on this book.

31 *Ad Momum.*

Momus thou say'st our verses are but toyes,
Tis true,yet truth is often spoken by boyes.

32 *On Thraso.*

Thraso goes lame with a blow he did receive,
In a late duell, if you'll him beleeve.

33 *News.*

When news doth come if any would discusse,
The letters of the word, resolve it thus:
News is convay'd by letter, word or mouth
And comes to us, from north,east,west and south

34 *Of Rufus.*

Rufus had robb'd his host and being put to it ;
Said I'm an arrant rogue , if I did doe it.

35 *Of Marcus.*

When *Marcus* fail'd a borrowed sum to pay ,
Unto his freind at the appointed day:
'Twere superstition for a man he sayes ,
To be a strict observer of set dayes.

36 *Of a theefe.*

A theefe arested and in custody ,
Under strong guards of armed company ,
Ask't why they held him so ? Sir quoth the cheife,
We hold you for none other than a theif.

37 *Of motion.*

Motion brings heat, and thus we see it prov'd
Most men are hot and angry , when they 're mov'd.

38 *Ad Scriptorem.*

Half of your book is to an index grown ,
You give your book *contents*, your reader none.

39 *Domi-*

✦✦✦✦✦✦✦✦✦✦✦✦✦✦✦✦✦✦✦✦✦✦✦✦✦✦✦

Domina Margarita Sandis :
39   Anagramma.
Anne domi das Margaritas ?

VVhy do wee feek & faile abroad to find,
Thofe pearls which do adorn the female-kind,
Within our feas there comes unto our hands,
A matchleffe Margaryte among the Sands.

40 *Man.*

Man's like the earth, his hair like graffe is grown,
His veins the rivers are, his heart the ſtone.

41 *Vita via.*

Well may mans life be likened to a way,
Many be weary of their life they 'll fay.

42 *To Mr. Thomas May.*

Thou fon of *Mercury* whofe fluent tongue
Made *Lucan* finifh his Pharfalian fong ,
Thy fame is equall, better is thy fate,
Thou haft got *Charles* his love, he *Nero's* hate.

43 *On*

43 *On Harpax.*

Harpax gave to the poor all by his will,
Becaufe his heir fhould no feign'd teares diftill.

44 *On Sextus.*

Sextus doth wifh his wife in heaven were
Where can fhee have more happines then there.

45 *To Mr. George Wythers.*

Th'haft whipp'd our vices fhrewdly and we may,
Think on thy fcourge untill our dying-day:
Th'haft given us a Remembrancer which fhall,
Outlaft the vices we are tax'd withall,
Th'haft made us both eternall, for our fhame
Shall never Wyther, whilft thou haft a name.

46 *On a Drawer drunk.*

rawer with thee now even is thy wine,
For thou haft peirc'd his hogs-head and he thine.

47 *Upon the weights of a clock.*

I wonder time's fo fwift, when as I fee,
Upon her heeles, fuch lumps of lead to bee.

48 *To*

¥¥¥¥¥¥¥¥¥¥¥¥¥¥¥¥¥¥¥¥¥¥¥¥¥¥¥¥¥¥¥¥¥¥¥

48 *To Mr. Thomas Middleton.*

Facetious *Middleton* thy witty Muse,
Hath pleafed all, that books or men perufe
If any thee difpife, he doth but fhow,
Antipathy to wit, in daring fo:
Thy fam's above his malice and 'twilbe,
Difpraife enough for him, to cenfure thee.

49 *On Cynna.*

Becaufe, I am not of a Giant's ftature,
Defpife me not, nor praife thy liberall nature,
For thy huge limbs, that you are great 'tis true,
And that I'm little in refpect of you,
The reafon of our growths is eas'ly had,
You many had perchance, I but one Dad.

50 *To Mr. James Shirly on his Comedy* viz. *the yong Admirall.*

How all our votes are for thee (*Shirly*) come
Conduct our troops, ftrike up Apollo's drum,
We wait upon thy fummons and do all,
Intend to choofe thee our yong Admirall:

51 *On*

51 *On Alastrus.*

Alastrus hath nor coyn, nor spirit nor wit,
I thinke hee's only then for Bedlam fit.

52 *On Macer.*

You call my verses toyes th' are so, 'tis true,
Yet they are better, then ought comes from you.

53 *To Mr. Philip Massinger.*

Apollo's *Messenger*, who doth impart
To us the edicts of his learned art,
We cannot but respect thee, for we know,
Princes are honour'd in their Legats so.

54 *On Celsus.*

Celsus doth love himself, *Celsus* is wise,
For now no rivall ere can claime his prize.

55 *On Candidus.*

When I am sick not else thou com'st to see me:
Waild fortune from both torments stillwould free
(me.
56 *To*

++++++++++++++++++++++++++++++++++++++

56 *To Mr. John Ford.*

If e're the Mufes did admire that well ,
Of Hellicon as elder times do tell ,
I dare prefume to fay upon my word ;
They much more pleafure take in thee rare *Ford*

57 *On Paulus.*

Becaufe thou followft fome great Peer at Court,
Doft think the world deem's thee a great one for
Ah no! thou art miftaken *Paulus,* know
Dwarfs ftill as pages unto giants goe.

58 *To Mr. Thomas Heywood.*

Thou haft writ much and art admir'd by thofe,
Who love the eafie ambling of thy profe ;
But yet thy pleafing ft flight , was fomewhat high
When thou did'ft touch the angels Hyerarchie :
Fly that way ftill it will become thy age ,
And better pleafe then groveling on the ftage.

59 *On a cowardly Souldier.*

Strotzo doth weare no ring upon his hand,
Although he be a man of great command ;

E

But gilded spurs do jingle at his heeles
Whose rowels are as big as some coach-wheels,
He grac'd them well, for in the Netherlands,
His heels did him more service then his hands.

60 To Mr. *Thomas Goffe on his tragedies.*

When first I heard the Turkish Emperours speak,
In such a dialect, and *Orestes* break
His silence in such language, I admir'd
What powerful savorite of the Nimphs inspir'd
Into their Souls such utterance, but I wrong,
To think 'twas learnt from any but thy tongue.

61 *On Cornuto.*

Cornuto is not jealous of his wife,
Nor e're mistrust's her too lascivious life,
Aske him the reason why he doth forbeare,
Hee'l answer straight, it commeth with a sear.

62 *On a Shrew.*

A froward shrew being blam'd because she show'd,
Not so much reverence as by right she ow'd
Unto her husband, she reply'd he might
Forbeare complaint of me, I do him right;

✦✦✦✦✦✦✦✦✦✦✦✦✦✦✦✦✦✦✦✦✦✦✦✦✦✦✦✦

His will is mine, he would beare rule, and I
Defire the like, onely in fympathy.

63 *On a youth married to an old woman.*

Fond youth I wonder why thou didft intend
To marry her who is fo neer her end ,
Thy fortune I dare tell, perchance thou'lt have
At fupper dainties ; but in bed a grave.

64 *On a dying Ufurer.*

With greater grief non doth death entertain,
Then wretched *Chryfalus*,he fighs a mayn,
Not that he dyes, but 'caufe much coft is fpent
Upon the Sexton and his regiment
The joviall ringers, and the Curate muft
Have his fee too, when duft is turn'd to duft ,
And which is greater then the former fum,
Hee'l pay an angell for a Moor-ftone-tomb.

65 *On a fly in a glaffe.*

A fly out of his glaffe a gueft did take,
E're with the liquor he bis thirft would flake ,
When he had drunk his fill,again the fly
Into the glaffe he put, and faid though I

Lov

Love not flyes in my drink, yet others may,
Whose humour I nor like, nor will gain-say.

66 On *Collimus.*

If that *Collimus* any thing do lend,
Or dog, or horse, or hawk unto his friend,
He to endear the borrowers love the more,
Saith he ne'r lent it any one before,
Nor would to any but to him : his wife
Having observ'd these speeches all her life,
Behind him forks her fingers and doth cry :
To none but you, I'd doe this courtesie.

67 *Auri-sacra fames-quia non?*

A smoothfac'd youth was wedded to an old,
Decrepit shrew, such is the power of gold :
That love did tye this knot, the end will prove,
The love of money not the god of love.

68 On *Sextus.*

What great revenews *Sextus* doth possesse,
When as his sums of gold are numberlesse,
What cannot *Sextus* have? I wonder then,
Sextus cann't live as well as other men.

C 2   69 *Good*

69 *Good wits jump.*

Againſt a poſt a ſcholler chanc'd to ſtrike,
At unawares his head, like will to like :
Good wits will jump (quoth he) if that be true
The title of a block-head is his due.

70 *On Womens Maskes.*

It ſeems that Masks do women much diſgrace,
Sith when they weare them they do hide their face

71 *On Lepidus and his wife.*

Lepidus married ſomewhile to a ſhrew,
She ſick'ned, he in jeſting wiſe to ſhew   (hear
How glad her death would make him; ſaid ſweet·
I pray you e're you ſing loath to depart
Tell who ſhall be my ſecond wife, and I
After your death will wed her inſtantly,
She ſomewhat vext hereat, ſtraightway reply'd,
Then let grim Pluto's daughter be your bride.
He anſwer'd wife I would your will obey,
But that our laws my willingneſſe gain-ſay:
For he who Pluto's ſiſter takes to wife,
Cannot his daughter too upon my life.

72 *Upon a pair of Tongs.*

The burnt child dreads the fire; if this be true,
Who first invented tongs it's fury knew.

73 *On Celſus his works.*

Celſus to pleaſe himſelfe, a book hath writ:
It ſeem's ſo, for there's few that buyeth it.
He is no popular man it thereby ſeems;
Sith men condemn, what he praiſe worthy deems,
Yet this his wiſdome and his book prefer,
Diſpraiſ'd by all, they think both ſingular.

74 *The Devill and the Fryar.*

The Devill was once deceived by a fryar,
Who though he ſold his ſoul cheated the buyer,
The devill was promiſt if he would ſupply,
The Fryar with coyn at his neceility,
When all the debts he ow'd diſcharg'd were quite,
The Devill ſhould have his ſoul as his by right,
The Devill defray'd all ſcores, payd all, at laſt,
Demanded for his due, his ſoul in haſte:
The Fryar return'd this anſwer, if I ow
You any debts at all, then you muſt know,

I am

I am indebted ſtill, if nothing be
Due unto you, why do you trouble me ?

75 *To Phillis.*

Aske me not *Phillis* why I do refuſe
To kiſſe thee as the moſt of gallants uſe,
For ſeeing oft thy dog to fawn and ſkip
Upon thy lap and joyning lip to lip,
Although thy kiſſes Iſull fain would crave;
Yet would I not thy dog my rivall have.

76 *Of Charidemus.*

Although thy neighbour have a handſom horſe,
Matchleſſe for comly ſhape, for hue and courſe
And though thy wife thou knoweſt ill-ſhapen be,
Yet *Charidemus* praiſes mightily,
His ugly wife and doth the horſe diſpraiſe :
How ſubtilly the fox his engin layes,
For he deſires his neighbours horſe to buy,
And ſell his wife to any willingly.

77 *Of Clytus.*

Clytus the barber doth occaſion fly,
Becauſe 'tis bal'd and he gains nought thereby.

78 On Balbus.

Balbus a verse on *Venus*, boy doth scan,
But ere 'twas finish'd *Cupid's* grown a man.

79 On Comptulus.

I wonder'd *Comptulus*, how thy long hair
In comely curles could show so debonair
And every hair in order be, when as
Thou could'st not trim it by a looking-glasse,
Nor any barber did thy tresses pleat,
'Tis strange; but Monsieur I conceive the feat
When you your hair do kemb, you off it take
And order't as you please for fashions sake.

80 On Gellius.

In building of his house, *Gellius* hath spent
All his revenews and his ancient rent,
Aske not a reason why *Gellius* is poor.
His great house hath turn'd him out of door.

81 To Ponticus.

At supper-time will *Ponticus* visit me,
I'd rather have his room then companie;

C 4

But

But if him. from me I can no wayes fright,
I'd have him visit me each fasting night.

82 *On a Pot-poet.*

What lofty verses *Cælus* writes? it is,
But when his head with wine oppressed is,
So when great drops of rain fall from the skyes
In standing pools, huge bubles will arise.

83 *On Onellus.*

Thou never supp'st abroad, *Onellus*, true;
For at my home I'm sure to meet with you.

84 *On Wine.*

What? must we then on muddy tap-lash swill,
Neglecting sack? which makes the poet's quill
To thunder forth high raptures, such as when
Sweet-tongued *Ovid* erst with his smooth pen,
In flourishing Rome did write; frown god of wine
To see how most men disesteem thy Vines.

85 *On beere.*

Is no juice pleasing but the grapes? is none,
So much beloved ? doth perfection,

Onely

Only conjoyn in wine? or doth the well
Of Aganippe with this liquor swell,
That Poets thus affect it? shall we crown,
A meer exotique? and contemn our own,
Our native liquor? haunt who list the grape,
Ile more esteem our Oate, whose reed shall make,
An instrument to warble forth her praise,
Which shall survive untill the date of daies,
And eke invoke some potent power divine,
To patronize her worth above the vine.

86 *On a vaunting Poetaster.*

Cæcilius boasts his verses worthy bee,
To be engraven on a Cypresse tree,
A Cypresse wreath befits 'em well; 'tis true,
For they are neer their death, and crave but due.

87 *On Philos.*

If *Philos*, none but those are dead, doe praise,
I would I might displease him all his dayes.

88 *On a valiant Souldier.*

A Spanish Souldier in the Indian war,
Who oft came off with honor and some scar,

After

After a tedious battle, when they were
Enforc'd for want of bullets to forbear,
Farther to encounter, which the Savage Moor
Perceiving, scoff'd, and nearer then before,
Approach'd the Christian host, the souldier grie
To be out brav'd, yet could not be reliev'd
Beyond all patience vex'd, he said although
I bullets want, my self will wound the foe;
Then from his mouth, took he a tooth and sent,
A fatall message to their regiment,
What armes will fury steed men with, when we.
Can from our selves have such artillery;
Sampson thy jaw-bone can no trophy reare
Equall to his, who made his tooth his speare.

89 *On Aurispa.*

Why doth the world repute *Aurispa* learn'd?
Because she gives men what they never earn'd.

90 *On Paulus.*

Those verses which thou mad'st I did condemn,
Nor did I censure thee in censuring them,
Thou mad'st them, but sith them in print I see,
They must the peoples not the authors bee.

91 *On Alexander the great.*

If *Alexander* thought the world but small
Becaufe his conquering hand fubdu'd it all,
He fhould not then have ftil'd himfelf the great,
An Infants ftool can be no giants feat.

92 *On a vertuous talker.*

If vertue's alwaies in thy mouth, how can
It ere have time to reach thy heart fond man?

93 *On a land-skip in the lid of his Mrs. Virginals.*

Behold Don *Phœbus* in yon fhady grove,
On his fweet harp plaies Roundelaies of love,
Mark how the fatyr grim *Marfyas* playes
On his rude pipe, his merry-harmleffe layes,
Mark how the fwaines attentively admire,
Both to the found of pipe and tang of lyre;
But if you on thefe Virginals will play,
They both will caft their inftruments away,
And deeming it the mufique of the Spheares
Admire your mufique as the fwains do theirs

94 *Upon pigs devouring a bed of penny-royall commonly called Organs.*

A good wife once a bed of Organs set,
The pigs came in and eate up every whit,
The good-man said wife you your garden may
Hogs Norton call, here pigs on Organs play.

95 *On a fortune-teller.*

The influence of the stars are known to thee,
By whom thou canst each future fortune see
Yet, sith thy wife doth thee a cuckold make,
'Tis strange they do not that to thee partake.

96 *On sore eyes.*

Fuscus was councell'd if he would preserve,
His eyes in perfect sight drinking to swerve;
But he replyd 'tis better that I shu'd
Loose them, then keep them for the worms as food

97 *On a gallant.*

A glittering gallant, from a prauncing steed,
Alighting down, desir'd a boy with speed

To

To hold his horse a while, he made reply ,
Can one man hold him faſt?'twas anſwerd I,
If then one man can hold him ſir, you may
Do it your ſelf, quoth he, and ſiunk away.

98 *On an inevitable Cuckold.*

Two wives th' haſt buried and another wed ,
Yet neither of the three chaſte to thy bed ,
Wherefore thou blam'ſt not onely them, but all
Their Sex into diſgrace and ſcorn doſt call,
Yet if the thing thou wilt conſider well ,
Thou wilt thy malice, and this rage expell ,
For when the three were all alike 't ſhould ſeem
Thy ſtars gave thee the Cuckold's anadem ,
If thou wert born to be a wittoll, can
Thy wife prevent thy fortune ? fooliſh man !
That woman which a *Hellen* is to thee ,
Would prove another mans *Penelope.*

99 *On an empty houſe.*

Lollus by night awak'd heard theeves about
His houſe, and ſearching narrowly throughout
To find ſome pillage there, he ſaid you may
By night, but I can find nought here by day.

✦✦✦✦✦✦✦✦✦✦✦✦✦✦✦✦✦✦✦✦✦✦✦✦✦✦✦✦✦

100 *On a bragging coward.*

Corfus in campe, when as his mates betook,
Themſelves to dine, encourag'd them, and ſpoke,
Have a good ſtomake Lads, this night we ſhall
In heaven at ſupper keep a feſtivall,
But battle joynd he fled away in haſte,
And ſaid I had forgot, this night I faſt.

101 *On a great noſe.*

Thy noſe no man wipe, *Proclus* unleſſe
He have a hand as big as *Hercules,* (heare,
When thou doſt ſneeze the found thou doſt not
Thy noſe is ſo far diſtant from thine eare.

102 *On an unequall paire.*

Faire *Phillis* is to churliſh *Priſcus* wed,
As ſtronger wine with waters mingled,
Priſcus his love to *Phillis* more doth glow;
With fervency then fire, her's cold as ſnow;
'Tis well for if their flames alike did burn,
One houſe would be to hot to ſerve their turn.

103 *On a changeable raiment.*

Know you why *Lollus* changeth every day,
His Perriwig, his face and his array,
'Tis not because his commings in are much,
Or cause hee'll swill it with the roaring dutch;
But 'cause the Sergeants (who a writ have had
Long since against him) should not know the lad.

104 *On the ensuring office.*

Linus met *Thuscus* on the burse by chance,
And swore he'd drink a health to th'heir of France
For on th'exchange for currant news 'twas told,
France had a Daulphin not yet seaven dayes old,
Thuscus excus'd himself, and said he must
By all meanes go to th'ensuring office first,
And so ensure some goods, he doubted were,
Unlikely else ere to his hands appeare,
Linus replyd Ile with thee then, for I
Would have my lands ensur'd to me in fee
Which otherwise I doubt, I never shall,
From debt and morgage ere redeem at all.

❖❖❖❖❖❖❖❖❖❖❖❖❖❖❖❖❖❖❖❖❖❖❖❖❖

105 *On a Tennis-court haunter.*

The world's a court, we are the bals, wherein
We bandied are by every ſtroke of ſin ,
Then onely this can I commend in thee ,
Thou acteſt well our frail mortalitie.

106 *On Baroſſa.*

*B*aroſſa boaſts his pedegree although ,
He knows no letter of the Chriſt-croſſe-row ,
His houſe is ancient, and his gentry great,
For what more ancient e're was heard of yet
Then is the family of fools, how than
Dare you not call *Baroſſa* gentleman ?

107 *On Clodius Albinus.*

Clodius great cheer for ſupper doth prepare,
Buyes Chickens, Rabbets, Pheſants and a hare ,
Great ſtore of fowl, variety of fiſh,
And tempting ſawce ſerv'd in, in every diſh,
To this great feaſt, whom doth he meane t' envite,
Albinus only ſups with him to night.

✦✦✦✦✦✦✦✦✦✦✦✦✦✦✦✦✦✦✦✦

108 *On Afer.*

Afer hath sold his land and bought a horse,
Whereon he prances into the royall Burse,
To be on horse back he delights, wilt know?
'Cause then his company hee'd higher show,
But happy chance tall *Afer* in his pride,
Mounts a Gunnell y and on foot doth ride.

109 *On Balbulus.*

Thou do'st complaine poets have no reward
And now adayes they are in no regard:
Verses are nothing worth, yet he that buyes,
Ought that is thine, at a three-farthings price,
Will think it too too dear, and justly may
Think verses are in price, since th' other day,
Yea who erebuies 'em at a farthings rate,
At the same price can never sell 'em at.

110 *To Lycus.*

That poetry is good and pleasing thou dost cry,
Yet know'it not when 'tis right or when awry
Thou know'st great *Ovid's* censure to abstaine
From pleasing good, is vertue's chiefest aime.

D

111 *On Charismus.*

Thou haft compos'd a book, which neither age
Nor future time fhall hurt through all their rage,
For how can future times or age invade
That work, which perifhed affoone as made.

112 *Of one praifing my book.*

Harpax doth praife my book I lately writ,
Saith it is fhort and fweet and full of wit ;
I knew his drift and fayd be filent 'pray ,
For in goodjfayth, I've given 'em all away.

113 *Facilis difcenfus averni.*

The way to hell is eafie, th' other day ,
A blind man thither quickly found the way.

114 *Age and Touth.*

Admire not youth, defpife not age, although
Some yong are grave, moft old men children grow

115 *On Orm.*

Orm fold wine, and then Tobacco, now
He Aqua-vitæ doth his friends allow,
What ere he had, is fold, to fave his life,
And now turn'd Pander he doth fell his wife.

116 *On Women.*

Women are books and men the readers be,
In whom oft times they great Errata's fee;
Here fometimes wee a blot, there wee efpy
A leafe mifplac'd, at leaft a line awry;
If they are books, I wifh that my wife were
An Almanacke to change her every yeare

117 *On Acerra.*

Tobacco hurts the braine phificians fay,
Doth dull the wit and memory decay,
Yet feare not thou *Acerra*, for 'twill ne'r
Hurt thee fo much by ufe, as by thy feare.

118 *On Brifo.*

Who private lives, lives well, no wonder then
You do abfent you from the fight of men,

❋❋❋❋❋❋❋❋❋❋❋❋❋❋❋❋❋❋❋❋❋❋❋❋❋❋

For out of doores you neer by day appeare,
Since laſt you loſt i'th pillory your eare.

119 *On the King of Swedens picture.*

Who but the halfe of this neat picture drew,
That it could ne're be fully done, well knew.

120 *To his Miſtris.*

Hyperbole of worth, ſhould wit ſuggeſt,
My will with Epithites, and I inveſt,
That ſhrine but with deſerved paraphraſe,
Adulatory poetry would praiſe.
And ſo but ſtaine your worth : your vertues (or
Elſe none at all) ſhall be my orator.

121 *B. J.* *anſwer to a thiefe bidding him ſtand.*

Fly villaine hence or be thy coate of ſteele,
Ile make thy heart, my brazen bullet feele,
And ſend that thrice as thieviſh ſoul of thine,
To hell, to weare the Devils Valentine.

122 *The Theefe's replie.*

Art thou great *Ben* ? or the revived ghoſt
Of famous *Shake-ſpear* ? or ſom drunken hoſt ?
Who

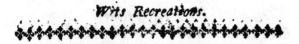

Who being tipsie with thy muddy beer,
Dost think thy rimes shall daunt my soul with fear
Nay know base slave, that I am one of those,
Can take a purse as well in verse as prose,
And when th' art dead, write this upon thy herse;
Here lies a Poet that was robb'd in verse.

123 *Upon Clarinda begging a lock of her lovers haire.*

Fairest *Clarinda*, she whom truth cals faire,
Begg'd my heart of mee, and a lock of haire
Should I give both said I, how should I live,
The lock I would, the heart I would not give,
For that lest theeving love should steal away,
Discretion had lock'd up and kept the key;
As for the locke of haire, which lovers use
My head laid on her knee I pray'd her chuse,
Taking her sizars by a cunning art,
First pick'd the lock, and then she stole my heart.

124 *To his Mistris.*

Dearest thy twin'd haires are not threds of gold,
Nor thine eyes diamonds, nor do I hold,
Thy lips for rubies, nor thy cheeks to bee,
Fresh roses, nor thy dugs of Ivory,

The skin that doth thy dainty body sheath,
Nor Alablaiter is, nor dost thou breath,
Arabian odours, these the earth brings forth,
Compar'd with thine, they would impair thy
Such then are other mistriffes, but mine, (worth;
Hath nothing earth, but all divine.

125 *The Answer.*

If earth doth never change, nor move,
There's nought of earth, sure in thy love,
Sith heavenly bodies with each one,
Concur in generation,
And wanting gravitie are light,
Or in a borrowed lustre bright;
If meteors and each falling star
Of heavenly matter framed are:
Earth hath my mistriffe, but sure thine
All heavenly is, though not divine.

126 *On his Mrs.*

I saw faire *Flora* take the aire,
When *Phœbus* shin'd and it was faire;
The heavens to allay the heat,
Sent drops of raine, which gently beat
The sun retires, asham'd to see
That he was barr'd from kissing thee

Then

Then *Boreas* took such high disdaine,
That soon he dri'd those drops again:
Ah cunning plot and most divine!
Thus to mix his breath with thine.

127 *On an houre glasse.*

Do thou consider this small dust
Here running in this glasse
    By atomes mov'd
Canst thou beleeve, that this the body was
    Of one that lov'd.
And in his Mistrisse playing like a fly
    Turn'd to cinders by her eye:
Yes and in death as life, have it exprest
    That lovers ashes take no rest.

128 *On the picture of Cupid in a jewell worn by his Mrs. on her brest.*

Little *Cupid* enter in and heat
Her heart, her brest is not thy seat;
Her brests are fitted to entice
Lovers, but her heart's of ice,
Thaw *Cupid*, that it hence forth grow
Tender still by answering no.

129

129 *On his Mistris.*

When first I saw thee thou didst sweetly play,
The gentle theefe, and stol'st my heart away;
Render me mine againe, or leave thy own,
Two are too much for thee since I have none;
But if thou wilt not I will swear thou art
A sweet-fac'd creature with a double heart.

130 *On Cupid.*

Cupid hath by his fly and subtill art,
A certaine arrow shot and peirc't my heart:
What shall I doe to be reveng'd on love?
There is but one way and that one I'le prove;
I'le steale his arrowes and will head them new,
With womens hearts and then they will fly true.

131 *On a Tobacconist.*

All dainty meats I do defie,
Which feed men fat as swine,
Hee is a frugall man indeed,
That on a leafe can dine,
He needs no napkin for his hands
His fingers ends to wipe,

That

That keeps his kitchin in a box
And roast-meat in a pipe.

132 *On the same.*

If mans flesh be like swines, as it is said
The metamorphosis is sooner made
Then full-fac'd *Gnatho* no tobacco take
Smoaking your corps; lest bacon you do make.

133 *Another.*

Tom I commend thee above all I know
That sold'st thy cushion for a pipe of To ———
For now tis like if ere thou study more,
Thou'lt sit to't harder then thou dist before.

124 *On Tobacco.*

Nature's Idea, phisicks rare perfection,
Cold rheumes expeller and the wits direction,
O had the gods known thy immortall smack,
The heavens ere this time had been colored black.

135 *On a beloved lye.*

I hate a lie, and yet a lye did run
Of noble *Goring's* death and *Kensington,*

           And

✦✦✦✦✦✦✦✦✦✦✦✦✦✦✦✦✦✦✦✦✦✦✦✦✦✦✦

And for that they did not untimely dye
I love a lye becaufe that was a ly ,
For had it been an accident of ruth
'T had made me grow in hatred of the truth,
Though lies be bad, yet give this lye it's due,
'Tis ten times better, then if 't had been true.

136 *On Button a Sexton, making a grave.*

Ye powers above and heavenly poles
Are graves become but *Button*-holes.

137 *On long haire.*

Lucas long haire down to his fhoulders weares,
And why ? he dares not cut it for his eares.

138 *A Crab's Reftorative.*

The Crab of the wood
Is fauce very good ;
    For the crab of the foaming fea,
But the wood of a Crab
Is fauce for a drab
    That will not her husband obey.

139 *On Juſtus Lypſius who bequeathed
his gown to the Virgin Mary.*

A dying latiniſt of great renown ,
Unto the Virgin *Mary* gave his gown
And was not this falſe latine, ſo to joyn
With femall gender, the caſe Maſculine.

140 *On a fidle-ſtick.*

Am I an inſtrument to make you ſport,
A fiddle-ſtick I am, ye ſhann't report
That ere yee hand'led me in ſuch a caſe ;
To make me ſtrike up fiddles mean and baſe ,
Nay you ſhall never bend me to your bow
It goeth againſt the haire you ſhould do ſo ,
Nor ſhall you curbe me in, thus every day,
I'le but my pleaſure, I was made to play;
But here I muſt not play upon another,
Why have I then a fiddle for my brother ?
If I were gon, you'd be compel'd my freinds
To make your muſique on your fingers ends :
My brother fiddle is ſo hollow hearted,
That ere't be long, we muſt needs be parted
And with ſo many frets he doth abound,
That I can never touch him but hee'l ſound :

When

When hee's reviv'd, this poore excuſe he puts,
That when I play, I vex him to the guts ;
But ſince it is my nature, and I muſt
I'le crowd and ſcrape acquaintance for a cruſt;
I am a genleman of high deſcent
Come from *Apollos* glorious element ,
Above the bridge I alwayes uſe to keep ,
And that's my proper ſpheare, when I do ſleep,
So that I cannot be in tune or town ,
For all my ſcraping if the bridge be down;
But ſince without an end, nought can endure,
A fiddle-ſtick hath two ends to be ſure.

141 *On hopes of preferment.*

I ſaw my fortune goe before
As *Palinurus* ſaw the ſhore,
If that I dye, before it hitch,
Wel-fare mine eyes for they are rich.

142 *Sorte tuâ contentus.*

If adverſe fortune bring to paſſe ,
And will that thou an aſſe muſt bee;
Then be an aſſe, and live an aſſe ,
For out of queſtion wiſe is hee
    That undergoes with humble mind,
    The ſtate that chance hath him aſſign'd.

141

143 *On a pretender to prophecy.*

Ninety two yeares the world as yet shall stand
If it do stand or fall at your command ;
But say why plac'd you not the world's end nigher
Lest ere you dy'd you might be prov'd a lyer.

144 *Mart. lib 8 epigr. 69.*

Old Poets only thou dost praise ,
   And none but dead one's magnifie :
Pardon *Vocerra*, thee to please ,
   I am not yet in mind to dye.

145 *On a Gamester.*

For hundred-thousands *Matho* playes ;
   Olus what's that to thee ?
Not thou by meanes thereof I trow ,
   But *Matho* poore shall bee.

146 *On Fr. Drake.*

Sir *Drake* whom well the world's end knew,
   Which thou did'st compasse round,
And whom both Poles of heaven once saw
   Which North and South do bound,

The

✠✠✠✠✠✠✠✠✠✠✠✠✠✠✠✠✠✠✠✠✠✠✠✠✠✠✠✠✠✠

The ſtars above, would make thee known,
 If men here ſilent were ;
The Sun himſelf cannot forget
 His fellow traveller.

147 *B. J. approbation of a copy of verſes.*

One of the witty ſort of gentlemen,
That held ſociety with learned Ben———
Shew'd him ſome verſes of ſuch Tragique ſenſe
They did his curious eare much violence ;
But after *Ben* had been a kind partaker
Of the ſad lines, he needs muſt know the maker ;
What unjuſt man he was, that ſpent his time
And baniſh'd reaſon to advance his rime :
Nay gentle *Ben*, replies the gentleman
I ſee I muſt ſupport the Poet than ;
Although thoſe humble ſtraines are not ſo fit
For to pleaſe you, hee's held a pretty wit ;
Is he held ſo? (ſaies *Ben*) ſo may a gooſe,
Had I the holding, I would let him looſe.

148 *On a gentleman that married an heire pri-*
vately at the Tower.

The angry Father hearing that his childe,
Was ſtoln, married, and his hopes beguild ;
       ('Cauſe

❧❧❧❧❧❧❧❧❧❧❧❧❧❧❧❧❧❧❧❧❧❧❧❧

('Cause his usurious nature had a thought
She might have bin to greater fortunes brought)
With rigid looks, bent brows, and words austere
Ask'd his forc'd son in law, how he did dare
(Without a full consenting from him carried)
Thus beare his onely daughter to be married,
And by what Cannons he assum'd such power?
He sayd the best in England sir, the Tower.

149 *A Gentlemans satisfaction for spitting in anothers face.*

A gentleman (not in malice nor disgrace,
But by a chance) spet in anothers face,
He that receiv'd it, knowing not the cause
That should produce such rashnes ('gainst the laws
Of Christian man-hood or civility)
In kindling anger, ask'd the reason why;
Pray sir sayes he, what thing that doth but sound
Like to an injury have you ere found
By me at any time? or if you had,
It never could deserve contempt so bad
'Tis an inhumane custome none cre use;
But the vile nation of contemned Jewes:
Pray sir, cryes th' other be not so unkind,
Thus with an accident to charge my minde
I meant it not, but since it fals out so,
I'm sorry, yea make satisfaction too;

                           Then

Then be not mov'd but let this ease your doubt
Since I have spet , please you, I'le tread it out.

150 *On a little Gentleman and one Mr. Story.*

The little man, by th' other mans vain-glory,
It seems was roughly us'd (so say's the story)
But being a little heated and high blown ,
In anger flyes at *Story*, puls him down,
And when they rise (I know not how it fated)
One got the worst, the *Story* was translated
From white to red, but ere the fight was ended
It seemes a Gentleman that one befriended
Came in and parted them; the little blade,
There's none that could intreat, or yet perswade,
But he would fight still, till another came ,
And with sound reasons councel'd gainst the same
'Twas in this manner friend ye shall not fight
With one that's so unequall to your height,
Story is higher, th' other made reply,
I'd pluck him down were he three *Stories* high.

151 *On a Welshman and an Englishman.*

There was a time a difference began
Between a Welshman and an Englishman,

And

And thus it was; the English-man would stand
Against all argument, that this our land,
Was freest of her fruits, there is a place
Quoth he, whose ground, so fruitfull is of grasse;
But throw a staffe in't but this night, you shall
Not see't the morrow, 't would be cover'd all:
The Welsh-man cry'd 'tis true, it might ly under,
The o're-grown grasse, wch is with us no wonder,
For turn your horse into our fruitfull ground,
And before morning come, he shann't be found.

152 *On a Souldier.*

The souldier fights well and with good regard,
But when hee's lame, he lies at an ill ward.

153 *On a faire Gentlewoman whose*
name was Brown.

We praise the faire, and our inventions wrack,
In pleasing numbers to applaud the black,
We court this Ladies eye, that Ladyes haire,
The faire love black, the black best like the faire,
Yet neither sort, I court, I doate upon
Nor faire nor black, but a complexion
More rare then either; she that is the crown
Of my entire affection is brown,

E   And

++++++++++++++++++++++++++++++++++

And yet fhees faire, 'tis ftrange, how can it be,
That two complexions fhould in one agree
Do I love *Brown*, my love can pleafe mine eye,
And fate my narrow'ft curiofity,
If I like faire, fhe hath fo fweet a grace,
That I could leave an Angell for her face,
Let any judge then, which complexion's rareft,
In my opinion, fhe is *Brown* that's faireft.

154 *On Garret and Chambers.*

Garret and his friend *Chambers* having done
Their Citty bus'neffe walk'd to Paddington,
And comming neer the fatall place where men
I meane offenders ne're return agen,
Looking on Tyborn in a merryment,
Sayes *Chambers* here's a pretty Tenement
Had it a garret: *Garret* hearing that,
Replyes friend *Chambers* I do wonder at
Your fimple cenfure, and could mock you for t
There muft be chambers ere there be a garret.

155 *On the word intollerable.*

Two gentlemen did to a Tavern come,
And call'd the drawer for to fhew a room,

Th

The drawer did, and what room think ye was't?
One of the small ones, where men drink in haste;
One gentleman sat down there, but the other
Dislik'd it, would not sit, call'd for another:
At which his friend, rising up from the table,
Cryes friend lets stay, this room is tollerable:
Why that's the cause (quoth hee) I will not stay,
Is that the cause, quoth th' other? why I pray?
To give a reason to you, I am able,
Because I hate to be in———Tollerable.

156 *Ad Lectorem.*

Is't possible that thou my book hast bought,
That saidst 'twas nothing worth? why was it
Read it again, perchance thy wit was dul,(naught
Thou may'st find something at the second pull,
Indeed at first thou nought didst understand,
For shame get somthing at the second hand.

157 *Suum cuique pulchrum.*

Posthumus not the last of many more,
Ask's why I write in such an idle vaine,
Seeing there are of Epigrams such store;
Oh give me leave to tell thee once again

That

****

That Epigrams are fitted to the feafon ,
Of fuch as beft know how to make rime reafo

158 *In magnis voluiſſe ſai eſt.*

In matters great to will it doth fuffice ,
I blufh to heare how loud this proverb lyes ,
For they that ow great fums by bond or bill,
Can never cancell them,with meere good will.

159 *As proud as witleſſe Draccus.*

Draccus his head is highly by him born ,
And fo by ftrawes are emptied heads of corne.

160 *S.liem videretur.*

A Welfhman and an Englifhman difputed ,
Which of their Lands maintain'd the greateft ftat
The Englifhman the Welfhman quite confuted,
Yet would the Welfhman nought his brags abate,
Ten cooks quoth he,in wales one wedding fees
Truth quoth the other, each man tofts his cheefe

161 *On womens inconstancy.*

Goe catch a ſtar that's falling from the skye,
Cauſe an immortall creature for to dye,
Stop with thy hand the current of the ſeas,
Poſte o're the earth to the Antipodes,
Cauſe times return and call back yeſterday;
Cloath January with the Month of May,
Weigh out an ounce of flame, blow back the wind
And then find faith within a womans mind.

162 *On Women.*

Why ſure theſe neceſſary harmes were fram'd,
That man as too too heedleſſe might be blam'd,
His weaknes cannot greateſt weakeneſſe fly,
In her ſtrong drawing, fraile neceſſity;
Then happy they, that know what women are,
But happier, which to know them never care.

163 *To his Mrs.*

Sweeteſt faire be not too cruell,
Blot not beauty with diſdaine,
Let not thoſe bright eyes adde fewell
To a burning heart in vaine,

E 3   Leaſt

Leaſt men juſtly when I dye
Deem you the candle, mee the fly.

164 *How to chooſe a wife.*

Good ſir, if you will ſhew the beſt of your skill;
    To picke a vertuous creature,
Then picke ſuch a wife, as you love a life,
    Of a comely grace and feature;
The nobleſt part let it be her heart,
    Without deceit or cunning,
With a nimble wit, and all things fit,
    with a tongue that's never running,
The haire of her head, it muſt not be red,
    But faire and brown as a berry;
Her fore-head high, with a chriſtall eye
    Her lips as red as a cherry.

165 *On his Miſtris.*

My love and I for kiſſes play'd,
She would keep ſtakes, I was content,
And when I wonne, ſhe would be payd;
This made me aske her what ſhe meant,
Sayth ſhe, ſince you are in this wrangling vaine,
Take you your kiſſes, and give me mine againe.

✦✦✦✦✦✦✦✦✦✦✦✦✦✦✦✦✦✦✦✦✦✦✦✦✦✦✦✦✦✦

166 *On a proud Mayde.*

She that will eate her breakfaſt in her bed,
And ſpend the morn in dreſſing of her head,
And ſit at dinner like a mayden-bride,
And talke of nothing all day but of pride,
God in mercy may doe much to ſave her,
But what a caſe is he in that ſhall have her?

167 *Satis eſt quod ſufficit.*

Weep no more, ſigh nor groane,
Sorrow recals not times are gone,
Violets pluck'd, the ſweetſt raine,
Makes not freſh or grow againe,
Joyes are windy, dreams flye faſt
Why ſhould ſadnes longer laſt?
Griefe is but a wound to woe,
Gentle faire, mourn no moe.

168 *Tempus edax rerum.*

Time eateth all things could the Poets ſay,
The times are chang'd our times drink all away.

❖❖❖❖❖❖❖❖❖❖❖❖❖❖❖❖❖❖❖❖❖❖❖❖

168 *Of women.*

Commit thy ship unto the winde,
But not thy faith to woman kind,
There is more safety in a wave,
Then in the faith that women have;
No woman's good, if chance it fall,
Some one be good amongst them all,
Some strange intent the dest'nies had,
To make a good thing of a bad.

169 *On a coy woman.*

She seems not won, yet won she is at length,
In loves war women use but half their strength.

170 *On Morcho.*

Morcho for hast was married in the night,
What needed day? his fair young wife is light.

171 *On Bed keeping.*

Bradus the smith, hath often sworn and sed,
That no disease should make him keep his bed;
His reason was, I oft have heard him tell it,
He wanted money therefore he would sell it.

172 *On a man stealing a candle from a lanthern.*

One walking in the street a winter-night,
Climb'd to a lanthern, thought t' have stole the
But taken in the manner and descri'd   (light,
By one o'th' servants who look'd out and cry'd,
Whose there? what d' you? who doth our lanthern
Nothing said he, but only snuf the candle. (handle,

173 *On Fraternus.*

Fraternus opinions show his reason weak
He held the nose was made for man to speak.

174 *On a french fencer, that challeng'd*
Church an English fencer.

The fencing Gaules in pride and gallant vaunt,
Challeng'd the English at the fencing skill,
The fencer *Church*, or the *Church* militant,
His errors still reprov'd and knock'd him still,
But sith our *Church* him disciplin'd so sore,
He (rank Recusant) comes to Church no more.

++++++++++++++++++++++++++++++++

175 *On two striving together.*

Two falling out into a ditch they fell,
Their falling out was ill, but in was well.

176 *On Musique.*

I want a quill out of an Angels wing,
To write sweet musike's everlasting praise,
I likewise want an Angels voice to sing
A wished anthem to her happy dayes,
    Then since I want an angels voice and pen,
    Let angels write and sing, I'le say amen.

177 *On Tobacco.*

Times great consumer, cause of idlenes,
Old whorehouse hunter, cause of drunkennes
Bewitching smoake, vainest wealths consumer;
Abuse of wit, stinking breath's perfumer,
Cause of entrailes blacknes, bodyes dyer
Cause of nature's slacknesse, quenching her fire,
Offence to many, bringing good to none,
Ev'n be thou hack'd till thou art burnt and gone.

178

178 *Claudianus de Sphærâ Archimedis*

When *Jove* within a little glaſſe ſurvay'd,
The heavens he ſmil'd, and to the Gods thus ſayd,
Can ſtrength of mortall wit proceed thus far?
Loe in a fraile orbe, my works mated are,
Hither the Syracuſians art tranſlates,   (fates
Heavens form, the courſe of things and humane
Th' including ſpirit ſerving the ſtar-deck'd ſignes
The living work inconſtant motion windes,
Th' adult'rate zodiaque runs a naturall yeere,
And *Cynthias* forg'd horns monethly new light
Viewing her own world, now bold induſtry(bear,
Triumphs and rules with humane power the sky.

179 *On Cælia.*

In *Cælia's* face a queſtion did ariſe,
Which were more beautifull her lips or eyes;
We ſay the eyes, ſend forth thoſe pointed darts,
Which pierce the hardeſt adamantine hearts,
From us reply the lips proceed thoſe bliſſes,
Which lovers reap by kind words and ſweet kiſſes
Then wept the eyes and from their eyes did pow'r
Of liquid Orientall pearle a ſhower,
Whereat the lips mov'd with delight and pleaſure
Through a ſweet ſmile unlock'd their Ivory trea-
                    ſure,   **And**

✦✦✦✦✦✦✦✦✦✦✦✦✦✦✦✦✦✦✦✦✦✦✦✦

And bad love judge, whether did ad more grace
Weeping or smiling pearls to *Celia's* face.

180 *On Chloris walking in the snow.*

I saw faire *Chloris* walke alone,
When feather'd raine came softly down,
Then *Jove* descended from his Tower,
To court her in a silver shower,
The wanton snow flew to her brest,
Like little birds into their nest ;
But overcome with whitenes there,
For greife it thaw'd into a teare,
Then falling down her garment hem,
To deck her, froze into a gem.

181 *To a Shoomaker.*

What bootes it thee, to follow such a trade,
That's alwaies under foot and underlaid ?

112 *Youth and Age.*

Age is deformed, youth unkind,
Wee scorn their bodies, they our mind.

183 *To Loquax.*

Loquax to hold thy tongue, would do thee wrong,
For thou would'st be no man, but for thy tongue.

184 *Death.*

The lives of men seem in two seas to swim,
Death comes to young folks and old goe to him.

185 *A disparity.*

Children fondly blab truth, & fools their brothers,
Women have learn'd more wisdom of their mo-
thers.

186 *To Makdist.*

Thou speakest ill, not to give men their dues,
But speakest ill, because thou canst not chuse.

187 *Womens properties.*

To weep oft, still to flatter, sometimes spin,
Are properties, women excell men in.

188 *Interpone tuis &c.*

Not mirth, nor care alone, but inter-wreathed,
Care gets mirth ftomacke, mirth makes care long
breathed

189 *Womens teares*

When women weep in their diffembling art,
Their teares are fauce to their malicious heart.

190 *Pot-Poets.*

Poet and pot differ but in a letter,
Which makes the Poet love the pot the better.

191 *Content.*

Content is all we ayme at with out ftore;
If that be had with little, what needs more.

192 *Faft and loofe.*

Paphus was marry'd all in hafte,
    And now to rack doth run;
So knitting of himfelf too faft,
    He hath himfelf undone.

193 *On Gervase.*

A double gelding *Gervase* did provide,
That he and 's wife to see their friends might side,
And he a double gelding prov'd indeed ;
For he so suddenly fell to his speed,
That both alight, with blows and threats among,
He leads him, and his wife drives him along.

194 *Tortus.*

Tortus accus'd to lye, to fawn, to flatter,
Said he but set a good face on the matter,
Then sure he borrow'd it for 'tis well known ;
Tortus ne're wore a good face of his own.

195 ANNAGRAMS·

Thomas Egerton,
1 anagr.
Honors met age.

Honors met age and seeking where to rest,
Agreed to lodge, and harbour in thy brest.

196 *On Captaine John,*
Came-age
2 anagr.
Age-came.

When perils I by land and sea had past,
Age came to summon me to death at last.

197 *Christopher Lindall,*
3 anagr.
I offer, lend Christ all.

That with this Epigram thy deeds agree,
They well know, that did ever well know thee.

198   *John Ryslen*
4 anagr.
In honors dy.

Thy actions friend declare thy noble mind ,
And to the world thy reall worth proclaime
That fame her self cannot thy equall find ,
To paralell thy glory and thy name ,
  On, onward still from no good action fly ,
  Who lives like thee, cann't but in honors dy.

199 *On the same.*

I nere will credit any powerfull fate ,
Can turn thy glory to a waning state,
Thou still wilt be thy self; therefore say I ,
Inhonors thou shalt live, but never dy.

200 *Phineas Fletcher.*
5 anagr.
Hath Spencer life ?
Or Spencer hath life.

That *Spencer* liveth, none can ignorant be,
That reads his works (*Fletcher*) or knoweth thee.

F   201

❧❧❧❧❧❧❧❧❧❧❧❧❧❧❧❧❧❧❧❧❧❧❧❧❧❧

201 *Mrs. Elizabeth Noell*
6 anagr.
holinesse be still my star.

The safest conduct to the port of blisse,
Lyes not in brittle honor, for by this
We often loose our way, to shun this bar,
To heaven, holines be still my star.

202 *My lot is blisse eternall.*

The world's a lottry, full of various chances,
Whereof each draws a share as fortune fancies,
A mong the rest that ayme at things supernall;
I've drawn, and find my lot is blisse eternall.

203 *I shall smite no ill brest.*

The common way to wound mens hearts I shun,
Nor with meere outside am I to be won,
Vertue may move me, for it crowns the best,
But I shall smite no ill or lustfull brest.

204 *My blisse on earth's little.*

Honors are faire but fading flowers which give,
Delight to those that gather them, but live

N

Not ever flowrifhing, this truth I find,
Too truely in my felfe, by fate affign'd
For having all, I fee that all's but but brittle,
And even at beft my bliffe on earth's but little.

205 *See my heart is ftill noble:*

Thongh fortune frowns and fate fuppres my will,
Yet fee the lucke, my heart is noble ftill.

206 *A riddle.*

Thoughts }
Searching } c

Valued } may B
Love

 Truth never eyes
Too A foole y y:
If have part

207 *Another being a translation.*

Est aliis servire tenetur
Jure· qui
  sum, servire necesse est
Jure tibi me
Te nulli cunctos
   ant   are videris
Qui cunctos hos laude
   ant   fero cunctis.

Thus Englished.

 -ling bound to serve his Mr's hands
An- is
 you -bound to do your high command
I'me and
None's you
 you all are then
I'le you
 -praise other men.

208 *Another.*

A begger once exceeding poore,
A penny pray'd me give him,

An

And deeply vow'd nere to aske more
And I ne're more to give him,
Next day he begg'd againe, I gave,
Yet both of us our oathes did save.

209 *Another.*

I hold as faith	What England's Church allows
What Rome's Church faith	My conscience disavowes
Where th' King is head	The Church can have no scame,
The Flocks misled	Where the Pope's supream
Where th' Alter's dreft	There's service scarce divine
The peopele's bleft	Where's table bread and wine
Hee's but an asse	Who the Communion flyes
Who shuns the Masse	Is Catholique and wise
Who charity preach	Their church with error's fraught
They heav'n soon reach	Where only faith is taught
On faith t' rely	No matter for good works
Is heresy	Make's Christians worse then Turks

210 *Another:*

There was a man befpake a thing,
Which when the owner home did bring,
He that made it, did refufe it,
He that bought it, would not ufe it,

F 3

He

✠✠✠✠✠✠✠✠✠✠✠✠✠✠✠✠✠✠✠✠✠✠✠✠✠

He that hath it doth not know
Whether he hath it, yea or no.

211 *On Women.*

Woman's the centre and the lines are men
The circles love, how doe they differ then?
Circles draw many lines into the center
But love gives leave to onely one to enter.

212 *On Clarret wine spilt.*

What's this that's spilt? 'tis clarret wine,
'Tis well 'tis spilt, it's fall sav'd mine.

213 *On womans love.*

A womans love is like a Syrian flower,
That buds and spreads and withers in an houre.

214 *On Cooke a cuckold.*

A young cooke marri'd upon Sunday last,
And hee grew-old e're tuesday night was past.

215 *A Butcher marrying a tanners daughter.*

A fitter match then this could not have bin,
For now the flesh is married to the skin.

216 *On Cupid.*

Cupid, no wonder was not cloath'd of old,
For love though naked seldom ere is cold.

217 *A plain sutor to his love.*

Faire I love thee, yet I cannot sue,
And shew my love as masking courtiers doe,
Yet by the smocke of *Venus* for thy good,
I'le freely spend my thrice concocted blood.

218 *On a passing bell.*

This dolefull musique of impartiall death,
Who danceth after, danceth out of breath.

219 *On a farmer knighted.*

In my conceit fir *John*, you were to blame,
To make a quiet goodwife a mad-dame.

220. *On Pallas and Bacchus birth.*

Pallas the offspring of *Jove's* braine,
Bacchus out of his thigh was ta'ne,
He breake's his braine that learning winns,
When he that's drunk breaks but his shins.

221 *On an old man doating on a yong wench.*

A rich old man loving a faire yong lasse,
Out of his breeches his spectacles drew,
Wherewith he read a note, how rich he was:
All which (quoth he.) sweet-heart I'le give to you
  Excuse me sir (quoth the for all your riches,
  Ile marry none, that wears his eies in's breeches

222 *Clownish Court-ship.*

Excellent Mrs. brighter then the moon,
Then scoured powter or the silver spoon,
Fairer then *Phœbus* or the morning star
Dainty fair Miſtriſſe by my troth you are,
As far excelling *Dian*, and her Nimphs,
As lobſters crawfiſh, and as crawfiſh ſhrimps.
Thine eyes like Diamonds do ſhine moſt cleerly
As I'm an honeſt man I love thee dearely.

223 *A Gentleman to his love.*

Tell her I love, and if she aske how well ;
Tell her my tongue told thee no tongue can tell*i*

224 *Her answer.*

Say not you love, unlesse you doe,
For lying will not honor you.

225 *His answer.*

Maddam I love, and love to doe,
And will not lye unlesse with you.

226 *On a Welshman.*

The way to make a welshman thinke on blisse,
And daily say his prayers on his knees,
Is to perswade him that most certaine 'tis,
The moon is made of nothing but green cheese,
Then hee'l desire of *Jove*, no geater boon,
Then to be pleas'd in heaven to eate the moon.

✦✦✦✦✦✦✦✦✦✦✦✦✦✦✦✦✦✦✦✦✦✦✦✦✦✦✦✦

227 *The vanity of man.*

That every thing we do, might vaine appeare,
We have a veine, for each day in the yeere.

228 *To a friend on the loſſe of his Mrs.*

If thou the beſt of women didſt forgo,
Weigh if thou found'ſt her, or didſt, make her ſo,
If ſhe was found, know there is more then one,
If made, the workman lives though ſhe be gone.

229 *On a whore.*

Roſa is faire, but not a proper woman,
Can any woman proper be that's common.

230 *On a Welſhman.*

A Welſhman comming late into an Inn,
Asked the maid what meat there was within
Cow-heels ſhe anſwered, and a breſt of mutton,
But quoth the Welſhman, ſince I am no glutton,
Either of both ſhall ſerve, to night the breſt,
The heels i'th morning, then light meat is beſt,
At night he tooke the breſt, and did not pay,
I'th' morning tooke his heels and run away.

231

231 *On men and women.*

I'll thrives that haplesse family, that showes
A cocke that's silent, and a hen that crows,
I know not which lives more unnaturall lives,
Obeying husbands or commanding wives.

232 *On Linus.*

Linus told me of verses that he made,
Riding to London on a trotting Jade,
I should have known, had he conceal'd the case,
Even by his verses of his horses pace.

233 *On a litle diminutive band.*

What is the reason of God-dam-me's band,
Inch-deep? and that his fashion doth not alter,
God-dam-me saves a labor, understand,
In pulling't off when he puts on the halter.

234 *On Julius.*

By fraud the Merchant *Julius* rakes in pelfe,
For heaven he sels, yet hath it not himself.

235 *On fine apparrell.*

Some that their wives may neat and cleanely go,
Do all their substance upon them bestow :
But who a goldfinch fain would make his wife,
Make's her perhaps a wag-taile all her life.

236 *Upon Conscience.*

Many men this present age dispraise ,
And thinke men have small conscience now adaie
But sure I'le lay no such fault to their charge ,
I rather think their conscience is too large.

237 *In Cornutum.*

Cornutus call'd his wife both whore and slut,
Quoth she, you'l never leave your brawling, but
But what quoth he ? quoth she the post or doore,
For you have horns to but, if I'me a whore.

238 *A witty passage*

An old man sitting at a Christmas feast ,
By eating Brawn occasioned a jest;
For whilest his tongue and gums chafed about,
For want of pales the chafed bore broke out,

An

And lights perchance upon a handsom lasse,
That neer him at the table placed was,
Which when she' spi'd she pluck'd out of her sleeve
A pin and did it to the old man give,   (slip,
Saying sith your brawn, out of your mouth doth
Sir take this pin and therewith close your lip,
And bursting into laughter, strain'd so much,
As with that strain her back-part spake low dutch
Which th' old man hearing, did the pin restore.
And bad her therewith close her postern doore.

239 *A new married Bride.*

The first of all our sex, came from the side of man
I thither am return'd from whence I came.

240 *On a pudding.*

The end is all , and in the end, the praise of all de-
              pends,
A pudding merrits double praise, because it hath
      two ends.

4t *Answer.*

A pudding hath two ends? you lye my brother,
For it begins at one, and ends at th' other.

242 *On maydes.*

Moſt maids reſemble *Eve* now in their lives,
Who are no ſooner women, then th' are wives,
As *Eve* knew no man ere fruit wrought her wo
So theſe have fruit oft e're their husbands know

243 *On a man whoſe choice was to be hang'd or married.*

M. Loe here's the bride, and here's the tree,
    Take which of theſe, beſt liketh thee.
R. The choiſe is laid on either part,
    The woman's worſe drive on the cart.

244 *Women.*

Were women as little, as they are good,
A peaſe cod would make them a gown and a hood.

245 *On a louſe.*

A louſe no reaſon hath to deal ſo ill,
With them of whom ſhe hath ſo much her will,
She hath no tongue to ſpeake ought in their praiſe,
But to back-bite them, finds a tongue all wayes.

246

246 *A Courtier and a Scholler meeting.*

A Courtier proud walking along the ſtreet,
Hap'ned by chance a Scholer for to meet, (place
The Courtier ſaid, (minding nought more then
Unto the Scholler meeting face to face,
To take the wall, baſe men Ile not permit,
The Scholler ſaid, I will, and gave him it.

247 *Cede majoribus.*

I took the wall, one rudely thruſt me by,
And told me the high way did open lye,
I thank't him that he would mee ſo much grace,
To take the worſe and leave the better place,
For if by owners we eſteem of things,
The wall's the ſubjects, but the way the kings.

248 *On Women.*

Are women Saints? no Saints, and yet no devils,
Are women good? not good, but needfull evils,
So angel like that devils you need not doubt,
Such needfull evils, that few can be without.

249 *On a Musitian and his Scholler.*

A man of late did his fair daughter bring
To a Musitian for to learne to sing,
He fell in love with her, and her beguil'd,
With flattering words and she was got with child,
Her Father hearing this was griev'd and said,
That he with her but a base-part had playd,
For wch he swore that he would make him smart
For teaching of his daughter such a part :
But the musitian said, he did no wrong,
He had but taught her how to sing prick-song.

250 *Why women weare a fall.*

A question 'tis why women weare a rau,
The truth it is to pride they are given all,
And pride the proverb saies must have a fall.

251 *Foras expertus.*

Priscus hath been a traveller, for why ?
He will so strangely swagger, swear and ly.

252 *Liber too wary to thrive.*

Liber is late set up, and wanteth custome,
Yet great resort hath got, but will not trust 'em:
Is not his love unto his friend the greater,
Hee'l want himselfe, ere hee'l see him a debtor.

253 *On Venus and Vulcan.*

I muse, why *Venus* hath such fiery holes,
I thinke that *Vulcan*, once there blow'd his coales.

254 *Detur quod meritum.*

A courtier kind in speech, curst in condition,
Finding his faults could be no longer hidden,
Came to his friend to cleare his bad suspition,
And fearing least he should be more then chidden.
Fell to flatt'ring and most base submission,
Vowing to kisse his foot if he were bidden.
    My foot said he? nay that were too submisse,
    You three foot higher, well deserve to kisse.

255

Gluto, at meales is never heard to talk,
For which the more his chaps and chin do walke,
G   Whet.

❖❖❖❖❖❖❖❖❖❖❖❖❖❖❖❖❖❖❖❖❖❖❖❖❖

When every one that fits about the bord,
Makes fport to aske; what *Gluto* ne're a word?
He forc'd to anfwer being very loath
Is almoft choak'd fpeaking and eating both.

256 *Sorte tua contentus.*

Birtus being bid to fupper to a Lord,
Was marfhall'd at the lower end of the boord,
Who vext thereat,'mongft his comrades doth fret
And fweares that he below the falt was fet;
But *Birtus*, t.i' art a fool to fret and fweare,
The falt ftands on the bord wouldft thou fit there

257 *Fovent perjuria furtum.*

Pifo hath ftoln a filver bole in jeft,
For which fufpected only, not confeft,
Rather then *Pifo* will reftore your bole,
To quit the body, he will caft the foule.

258 *The promife breaker.*

Ventus doth promife much,but ftill doth breake,
So all his promifes are great and weake;
Like bubbles in the water(round and light)
Swelling fo great, that they are broke out-right

259 *Nummos & demona jungit.*

Bat bids you swell with envy till you burst,
So he be rich, and may his coffers fill,
Bringing th' example of the fox that's curst,
And threatning folks who have least power to kill:
  For why 'tis known, his trade can never fall,
  That hath already got the devill and all.

260 *Nil gratum ratione carens.*

Paulus a pamphlet doth in prose present,
Unto his lord, (the fruits of idle time)
Who farre more carelesse then therewith content,
Wisheth it were converted into rime:
Which done and brought him at another season,
Sayd now 'tis rime, before nor rime nor reason.

261 *Non cessat perdere lusor.*

Aske *Ficus* how his lucke at dicing goes.
Like to the tide (quoth he) it ebbs and flowes,
Then I suppose his chance cannot be good,
For all men know, 'tis longer ebbe then flood.

262 *Vulnerem sic decipit anceps.*

Hidrus the horse-courser(that cunning mate)
Doth with the buyers thus equivocate,
Claps on his hand, and prayes he may not thrive
If that his gelding be not under five.

263 *Perdat qui caveat emptor.*

Nor lesse meant *Promus* when that vow he made,
Then to give ore his cous'ning tapsters trade,
Who check'd for short and frothy measure, swore
He never would from thence forth fill pot more.

264 *Virescit vulnere Venus.*

Susan's well sped and weares a velvet hood,
As who should know, her breeding hath bin good,
'Tis reason she should rise once in her life,
That fell so oft before she was a wife.

265 *On Death.*

How base hath sin made man, to feare a thing
Which men call *Mors?* which yet hath lost all sting

And

And is but a privation as we know,
Nay is no word, if wee exempt the O,
Then let good men the feare of it defie,
All is but O when they shall come to dye.

266 *On a rich country Gentleman.*

Of woods, of plaines, of hils and vales,
Of fields, of meades, of parks and pales,
Of all I had, this I possesse,
I need no more I have no lesse.

267 *On his Mrs.*

Shall I tell you how the rose at first grew red,
And whence the lilly whitenes borrowed,
You blusht, &straight the rose with red was dight,
The lilly kist your hand, and so was white,
Before such time, each rose had but a stain,
And lillies nought but palenes did contayne,
You have the native colour, these the dy,
And onely flowrish in your livery.

268 *To his Mrs.*

Think not deare love that I'le reveale,
Those houres of pleasure we do steale,

No eye shall see, nor yet the sun,
Descrie what thee and I have done;
The God of love himself, whose dart
Did first peirce mine, and next thy heart,
He shall not know, that we can tell
What sweets in stoln embracements dwell,
Onely this meanes may find it out,
If when I dy, Phisians doubt
What caus'd my death and they to view
Of all the judgements that are true,
Rip up my heart oh then I feare,
The world will find thy picture there.

269. *To Mr. Ben. Johnson demanding the rea-*
son why he call'd his playes works.

Pray tell me *Ben,* where doth the mistery lurke,
What others call a play you call a worke,

270. *Thus answer'd by a friend in Mr.*
Johnsons defence.

The authors friend thus for the author sayes,
Bens plays are works, when others works are plaies

271 *Tempus edax rerum.*

The sweetest flower in the summers prime,
By all agreement is the damaske rose,
Which if it grow, an' be not pluck'd in time,
She sheds her leaves her buds their sent do loose,
   Oh let not things of worth, for want of use
   Fall into all consuming times abuse:
The sweetest work that ever nature fram'd,
By all agreement is a virgins face,
Which not enjoy'd, her white and red will fade,
And unto all worm eating time give place:
   Oh let not things of worth, for want of use
   Fall into all consuming times abuse.

272 *Ad Aristarchum.*

Be not agriev'd my humerous lines afford,
Of looser language here and there a word,
Who undertakes to sweep a common sinke,
I cannot blame him, though his broome do stinke.

273 *To his Mrs.*

Thou send'st to me a heart was Crown'd,
I tooke it to be thine,
But when I saw it had a wound,
I knew that heart was mine.

A

A bounty of a ftrange conceit,
To fend mine own to me,
And fend it in a worfe eftate,
Then when it came to thee;
The heart I gave thee had no ftaine,
It was intire and found;
But thou haft fent it back againe,
Sick of a deadly wound.
Oh heavens! how wouldft thou ufe a heart
    That fhould rebellious be,
When thou haft kill'd me with a dart,
    That fo much honor'd thee.

274 *On a charming beauty.*

I'le gaze no more on that bewitched face,
Since ruin harbors there in every place,
For my inchanted foul alike fhe drowns,
With calms and tempefts of her fmiles and frowns
I'le love no more thofe cruell eyes of hers,
Which pleas'd or anger'd ftill are murtherers,
For if fhe dart like lightning through the ayre,
Her beames of wrath, fhe kils me with defpaire,
If fhe behold me with a pleafing eye,
I furfet with exceffe of joy and dy.

275 *Covetous persons.*

Patrons are latrons, then by this,
Th' are worst of greedy people,
Whose cognizance a wolfes head is,
And is his mouth a steeple.

276 *On a dyer.*

Who hath time hath life, that he denies,
This man hath both, yet still he dyes.

277 *Non verbera sed verba.*

Two Schollers late appointed for the field,
Must, which was weakest to the other yeeld,
The quarrell first began about a word,
Which now should be decided by the sword;
But er'e they drew, there fell that alteration,
As they grew friends againe by disputation.

278 *In Octavium.*

Octavius lying at the point of death,
His gelding kindly did to me bequeath:
I wanted one, and was in haste to ride,
In better time he never could have di'd.

279

279 *Of letting.*

In bed a yong man with his old wife lay,
O wife quoth he I've let a thing to day,
By which I feare I am a loofer much:
His wife replyes youths bargaines ftill are fuch;
So turning from him angry at her heart,
She unawares let out a thundring———
Oh wife quoth he, no loofer I am now,
A marv'lous faver I am made by you:
Yong men that old wives have may never fell,
Becaufe old wives quoth he let things fo well.

280 *In Doſſum.*

Doſſe riding forth the wind was very big
And ftrained court'fie with his perriwig,
Leaving his fconce behind fo voyd of haire,
As Efops crow might breake her oyfter there;
Foole he to thinke his haire could tarry faft,
When *Boreas* teares up forefts with a blaft.

281 *Poft dulcia finis amarus.*

Jenkin a welfh-man that had fuires in law,
Journying to London chanc'd to fteale a cow;

For which (pox on her luck as ne're man saw)
Was burnt within the fist, and know not how :
    Being ask'd if well the lawes with him did stand
    Was have her now (quoth *Jenkin*) in her hand.

282 *In Mincam.*

Fine *Minca* lisping yea and no forsooth,
Though little eats, yet keeps a dainty tooth :
Minca that longs for apples on the tree,
In May, before the blossomes fallen be,
Or will not eate a Kentish cherry down ,
But for a couple, when she payes a crown,
And cares not for a straw-berry or peare ,
In truth because th' are common every where,
Yet what is that which may be had for reason,
And never comes to *Minca* out of season ?

283 *Femina ludificantur viros.*

Kind *Katherine* to her husband kist these words,
Mine own sweet *Will* how dearly do I love thee ?
If true (quoth *Will*) the world no such affords ,
And that it's true I durst his warrant bee,
    For ne're heard I of woman good or ill ,
    But alwayes loved best her own sweet will.

284

284 *Ad Tusserum.*

Tusser, they tell me when thou wert alive,
Thou teaching thrift, thy self couldst never thriv
So like the whetstone many men are wont
To sharpen others when themselves are blunt.

285 *Præstat videri quam esse.*

Clitus with clients is well customed,
That hath the laws but little studied;
No matter *Clitus* so they bring their fees,
How ill the case and thy advice agrees.

286 *Tunc tua res agitur.*

A jealous merchant that a saylor met,
Ask'd him the reason why he meant to marry,
Knowing what ill their absence might beget,
That still at sea, constrained are to tarry?
Sir (quoth the Saylor) think you that so strange!
'Tis done the time whiles you but walke th' ex-
(change

287 *A conference.*

A Dane, a Spaniard, a Polonian,
My selfe, a Swisse, with a Hungarian,

A

At supper met difcourfed each with other,
Drank, laught, yet none that underftood another.

288 *In Marcum.*

Marcus is not a hypocrite and why?
He flyes all good, to fly hypocrifie.

289 *Quid non verba fuadeant.*

Sextus, halfe falv'd his credit with a jeft,
That at a reckoning this devife had got,
When he fhould come to draw amongft the reft,
And faw each man had coine, himfelfe had not;
   His empty pocket feels and 'gins to fay,
   In fadnes firs here's not a croffe to pay.

290 *Stupid Binus.*

Sith time flyes faft away, his fafteft flight,
Binus prevents with dreaming day and night.

291 *In divites.*

Rich men their wealth as children rattles keep,
When playd a while with't then they fall afleep.

✚✚✚✚✚✚✚✚✚✚✚✚✚✚✚✚✚✚✚✚✚✚✚✚✚✚✚

292 *In Fannium.*

What furi's this,his foe'whilſt *Fannius* flyes,
He kils himſelf, for feare of death he dies.

293 *To Vellius.*

Thou ſweareſt I bowle as well as moſt men doe,
The moſt are bunglers, therein thou ſay'ſt true.

294 *In divites iracundos.*

Rich friends 'gainſt poore to anger ſtill are prone,
It is not well but profitably done.

295 *Clericus abſque libro.*

When *Craſſus* in his office was inſtal'd,
For ſumms of money, which he yet doth ow,
A client by the name of Clerk him call'd,
As he next day to Weſtminſter did go,
Which *Craſſus* hearing whiſpers thus in's eare,
Sirrah you now miſtake and much do erre,
That henceforth muſt the name of Clerke forbear,
And know I am become an officer.
  Alas (quoth he) I did not ſo much marke,
  Good Mr. officer, that are no clerke.

296 *Durum telum neceſſitas.*

Coquus with hunger pennileſſe conſtrain'd
To call for meat and wine three ſhillings coſt,
Had ſuddainly this project entertain'd;
Inſtead of what's to pay, to call mine hoſt,
Who being come entreateth him diſcuſſe;
What price the law allots for ſhedding blood:
Whereto mine hoſt directly anſwers thus,
'Twas alwayes fourty pence he underſtood;
   So then quoth *Coquus* to requite your paines
   Pray break my head, & give me what remaines.

297 *Loves Lunacy.*

Before I knew what might belong to war,
I was content to ſuffer many a ſcar;
Yet none could hurt me,'till at length a boy,
Diſgrace to manhood, wrought my ſad annoy,
This lad though blind, yet did he ſhoot a dart
Which pierc'd my breſt and lighted on my heart,
Yet did I feel no hurt till from above,
I heard a voyce ſay ſouldiers you muſt love,
I lik't it well and in this pleaſing vaine :
I loſt my wits to get my heart againe.

﹢﹢﹢﹢﹢﹢﹢﹢﹢﹢﹢﹢﹢﹢﹢﹢﹢﹢﹢﹢﹢﹢

298 *Se his Mrs.*

Your lips(faire Lady)(ift be not too much,
I beg to kiffe, your hand I crave to touch,
And if your hand deny that courtefie,
(Sweet Miftris) at your feet I proftrate ly;
But if your foot Spurn my humility,
Or that your lips think I do aime too high:
Then let your hand in token of confent,
Point at the meane, the maine of all content,
And I fhall leave extreames, and to be blift,
Reft in your midft where vertue doth confift.

299 *To an upftart.*

Thine old frinds thou forgot'ft having got weald
No marvaile, for thou haft forgot thy felf.

300 *Suum euique.*

A ftrange contention being lately had
Which kind of Muficke was the fweet'ft and beft,
Some prais'd the fprightly found and fome the fad
Some lik't the viols; and among the reft
Some in the bag-pipes commendations fpoke,
(Quoth one ftood by) give me a pipe of fmoake.

301

301 *Similis doctrina libello.*

Crasus of all things loveth not to buy
So many books of such diversity :
Your Almanack (sayes he) yeeld's all the sence,
Of time's best profit and experience.

302 *On Tullus.*

Tullus who was a Taylour by profession,
Is late turn'd Lawyer, and of large possession.

303 *In Prodigum.*

Each age of men new fashions doth invent,
Things which are old, young men do not esteeme :
What pleas'd our fathers doth not us content
What flourish'd then we out of fashion deeme.
   And that's the cause as I doe understand,
   Why Prodigus did sell his fathers land.

304 *In medicum.*

When Mingo cryes how doe you sir ? tis thought,
His Patient's wanteth and his Practice's naught :
Wherefore of late, now every one he meeteth,
With I am glad to see you well——he greeteth :

H   But

But who'l beleeve him now, when all can tell,
The world goes ill with him, when all are well,

305 *Crispati crines plumæ dant calcar amori,*

Why is young *Annus* thus with feathers dight ?
And on his shoulder weares a dangling lock ?
The one foretels hee'l sooner fly then fight,
The other showes hee's wrapt in's mothers smock
  But wherefore weares hee such a jingling spur
  O know, he deales with jades that will not stir

306 *Most men mistaken.*

Good, bad, rich, poor, the foolish and the sage,
Doe all cry out against the present age :
Ignorance make us thinke our young times good
Our elder dayes are better understood :
Besides griefes past, we easily forget,
Present displeasures make us sad or fret.

307 *On Glaucus.*

Glaucus a man, a womans hayre doth weare,
But yet he weares the same comb'd out behinde :
So men the wallet of their faults doe beare,
For if before him, he that fault should finde :

I thinke foule shame, would his fayre face invade,
To see a man so like a woman made.

308 *Of Batardus.*

Batardus needs would know his Horoscope,
To see if he were borne to scape the rope :
The *Magus* said, ere thou mine answer have,
I must the names of both thy parents crave :
That said, Batardus could not speak, but spit;
For on his fathers name he could not hitt :
And out of doores at last he stept with shame,
To aske his mother for his fathers name.

309 *An idle huswife.*

Fine, neat, and curious misteris Butterfly,
The idle toy, to please an idiots eyes :
You, that wish all good huswives hang'd, for why,
Your dayes work's done, each morning as you rise :
Put on your gown, your ruff, your mask, your chain,
Then dine and sup, and goe to bed againe.

310 *Consuetudo lex.*

Two Woers for a Wench were each at strife,
Which should enjoy her to his wedded wife :

Quoth

Quoth th' one, fhee's mine, becaufe I firft her faw,
Shee's mine quoth th'other by Pye-corner law :
Where fticking once a pricke on what you buy,
It's then your owne, which no man muft deny.

311 *In Battum.*

Battus affirm'd no Poet ever writ,
Before that love infpir'd his dull-head witt :
And that himfelfe in love, had wit no more,
Then one ftarke mad,though fomewhat wife befor

312 *To women.*

You were created angels pure and fayre,
But fince the firft fell, tempting devills you are:
You fhould be mens bliffe,but you prove their rod
Were there no women men might live like gods,

313 *On marriage.*

Wedding and hanging the deftinies difpatch,
But hanging to fome, feemes the better match.

314 *Quidam erat.*

A preaching fryar there was, who thus began,
The fcripture faith there was a certaine man :

A certain man ? but I do read no where,
Of any certaine woman mention'd there :
A certaine man a phrase in scripture common,
But no place shewes there was a certaine woman :
And fit it is, that we should ground our faith,
On nothing more then what the scripture saith.

315 *Against a certaine——*

For mad-men Bedlam, Bridewell for a knave,
Choose whether of those two, th' hadst rather have.

316 *Loves progresse.*

Loves first approach, delights sweet song doth sing,
But in departure, shee woes stinge doth bring.

417 *On old Scylla.*

Scilla is toothlesse, yet, when shee was young,
Shee had both teeth enough and to much tongue:
What shall I then of toothlesse *Scilla* say,
But that her tongue hath worne her teeth away.

318 *On Gallants Cloakes.*

Without,plaine cloth, within, plufh't?but I doubt
the wearers worft within, and beft without.

319 *On Banks the ufurer.*

Banks feels no lameneffe of his knotty gout,
His monyes travaile for him in and out :
And though the foundeft legges go every day,
He toyles to be at hell as foone as they.

320 *Pecunia prævalens.*

Tell *Tom* of *Plato's* worth or *Ariftotles* ?
Hang't give him wealth enough,let wit ftop bottle.

321 *On the fame.*

Tom vow'd to beat his boy againft the wall,
And as he ftrucke, he forth-with caught a fall :
The boy deriding faid,I doe averre,
Y' have done a thing, you cannot ftand to fir.

322 *On debt.*

To be indebted is a fhame men fay,
Then' tis confeffing of a fhame to pay.

323 *Umbras non certus metuit*

Miſtriſſe *Maryna* ſtarts to ſee a frog,
A naked rapier or a creeping mouſe :
To hear a Gun, or barking maſtive dog,
Or ſmell Tobacco, that defiles her houſe,
   To taſte of fiſh, no man alive ſhall wooe her,
   Yet feares ſhe not what fleſh can doe unto her.

324 *On women.*

Although they ſeeme us onely to affect,
'Tis their content, not ours, they moſt reſpect :
They for their own ends cunningly can feigne,
And though they have't by nature, yet they'll ſtrain :
Sure if on earth, by wiles gain'd might be bliſſe,
Staight that I were a woman I would wiſh.

325 *On Soranzo.*

Soranzos broad-brim'd hat I oft compare,
To the vaſt compaſſe of the heavenly ſpheare :
His head, the earths globe, fixed under it,
Whoſe center is, his wondrous little witt.

326 *In Cottam.*

Cotta when he hath din'd faith god be prais'd,
Yet never prayfeth god, for meat or drinke:
Sith *Cotta* fpeaketh and not practiceth,
He fpeaketh furely what he doth not thinke.

327 *De corde & lingua.*

The tongue was once a fervant to the heart,
And what it gave thee freely did impart :
But now hypocrifie is growne fo ftronge:
Shee makes the heart a fervant to the tongue.

328 *On poverty.*

If thou be'poor, thou fhalt be ever fo.
None now doe wealth but on the rich beftow.

329 *Women are mens fhadowes :*

Follow a fhaddow it ftill flies you,
Seeme to fly, it will purfue :
So court a miftriffe fhee denies you,
Let her alone, fhe will court you.
   Say are not women trnely then,
   Stil'd but the fhadwoes of us men ?

At

At morne and even ſhades are longeſt,
At noone they are, or ſhort or none :
So men at weakeſt they are ſtrongeſt ;
But grant us perfect they're not known.
  Say are not women truely then
  ſtil'd but the ſhadowes of us men ?

330   *In ebrioſum.*

Fy man (ſaith ſhee) but I tell miſtriſſe *Anne,*
Her drunken husband is no drunken man :
For thoſe wits, which are overcome with drink,
Are voyd of reaſons and are beaſts I thinke.

331   *Wills errour.*

Will ſayes his wife's ſo fat, ſhee ſcarce can goe,
But ſhee as nimbly anſwers ſaith ſir no :
Alas good *Will* thou art miſtaken quite,
For all men know, that ſhee is wondrous light.

332   *On Rome.*

Hate & debate *Rome* through the world hath ſpred,
Yet *Roma* a.... ckeward read :

                              Then

Then is't not strange, *Rome* hate should foster ? no,
For out of backward love all hate doth grow.

333

All things have favour, though some very small,
Nay a box on the eare hath no smell at all.

334   *Art, fortune, and ignorance.*

When Fortune fell asleep, and Hate did blinde her,
Art Fortune lost, and Ignorance did finde her:
Sith when, dull Ignorance with Fortune's store,
Hath bin enrich'd and Art hath still bin poore.

335   *On Ebrio.*

See where *Don Ebrio* like a Dutch-man goes,
Yet drunke with Englif ale; one would suppose:
That he would shoulder down each door & wall,
But they must stand, or he, poor fool! must fall :

336   *On love.*

Love hath two divers wings, as lovers say,
Thou following him, with one he flies away :

With

With th' other, if thou fly, he followes thee,
Therefore the laſt, Love, onely uſe for me.

337 *On the ſame.*

Love, as tis ſaid, doth work with ſuch ſtrange tools,
That he can make fooles wiſe-men, wiſe-men fools :
Then happy I, for being nor foole nor wiſe,
Love with his toyes and tooles I ſhall deſpiſe.

338 *On a wanton.*

Some the word wanton fetch, though with ſmal skil
From thoſe that want one to effect their will :
If ſo, I thinke that wantons there are none,
For till the world want men, can they want one ?

339 *In procos :*

Who woes a wife, thinks wedded men do know,
The onely true content, I thinke not ſo :
If Woe in wooers bee, that women court,
As the word Woe in wooers doth import :
And Woe in woemen too, that courted be,
As the word Woe, in women we doe ſee :

I thinke 'tis better lead a single life,
Then with this double woe to wooe a wife.

340 *Ingluviem sequitur fames :*

Curio would feed upon the daintyest fare,
That with the court or countrey might compare:
For what let's *Curio* that he need to care,
To frolique freely with the proud'st that dare :
   But this excesse was such in all things rare,
   As he prov'd banquerout e're he was aware.

341 *In Corbum.*

Corbus will not, perswade him all I can,
The world should take him for an gentleman :
His reason's this, because men should not deeme,
That he is such, as he doth never seem.

342 *On Priscus mistrisse.*

Priscus commends his mistrisse for a girle,
Whose lips be rubies, and whose teeth are pearl :

Th'had

Th' had need prove so, or else it will be found,
He payes too deare ; they cost him many a pound.

343 On Women.

Women thinke wo——men far more constant bee,
Then wee men, and the letter O wee see :
In wo——men, not in we men, as they say,
Figures earth's constant Orbe ; we men say nay :
It meanes the moone, which proves (none thinke it
women are constant, & most true in cha..ge (strange

344 On Promises.

My Mistrisse sweares shee'd leave all men for me,
Yea though that *Jove* himselfe should rivall be :
Shee sweares it, but what women sweare to kind-
-Loves, may be writ in rapid seas and winde.

345 To his mistrisse.

Take, oh take those lips away,
That so sweetly were for-sworne :
And those eies like breake of day.
Lights that doe mislead the morne :
  But my kisses bring againe,
  Seales of love, though seal'd in vaine.

Hide

Hide, oh hide thofe hills of fnow,
Which thy frozen bofome beares :
On whofe tops the pinkes that grow,
Are of thofe that Aprill weares :
    But firft fet my poor heart free,
    Bound in thofe icie chaines by thee.

346 *On fouldiers.*

Not faith, nor confcience common fouldiers carry,
Beft pay, is right ; their hands are mercinary.

347 *In Diogenem & Crafum :*

When the tubb'd *Cynicke* went to hell, and there,
Found the pale ghoft of golden *Crafus* bare,
Hee ftops ; and jeering till he fhrugges againe,
Sayes O ! thou richeft king of kings, what gaine
Have all thy large heapes brought thee, fince I fpie
Thee here alone, and poorer now then I ?
For all I had, I with me bring ; but thou,
Of all thy wealth haft not one farthing now.

348 *On a barber.*

Suppofe my Barber, when his razors nigh
My throat, fhould then aske wealth and liberty :
                I'de

Ide promise sure, the Barber askes not this,
No, tis a Thiefe and feare imperious is.

349 *Drusius and Furio.*

Furio would fight with *Drusius* iu the field,
Because the Straw, stout *Drusius* would not yeeld,
On which their mistrisse trod, they both tid meet,
Drusius in fight fell dead at *Furios* feet,
One had the Straw, but with it this greek letter
The other lost it, pray who had the better?

350 *On Cupid.*

Love is a boy, and subject to the rod
Some say, but lovers say he is a god :
I thinke that love is neither god nor boy,
But a mad-braines imaginary toy.

351 *On Durus.*

A friend of *Durus* comming on a day
To visite him, finding the doores say nay ;
Being lock'd fast up, first knocks, and then doth
As Lord have mercy on's had bin the cause; (Pause,

But

But miffing it, he ask't a neighbour by
When the rich *Durus* were lock'd and why?
He faid it was a Cuftome growne of late
At dinertime to lock your great man's gate.
Durus his poor friend admir'd & thought the dore
Was not for State lock'd up, but 'gainft the poore
And thence departing empty of good cheere,
Said, Lord have mercy on us, is not there.

352. *On a Puritane.*

From impure mouthes now many bear the name
Of Puritane, yet merit not the fame,
This one fhall onely be my Puritan
That is a knave, yet feems an honeft man.

353. *Quantum mutatus ab illo.*

Pedes growne proud makes men admire thereat
Whofe bafer breeding, fhould they think not bet
Nay,he on cock-horfe rides,how like you that? (it
Tut *Pedes* Proverb is, Win gold and wear it,
But *Pedes* you have feen them rife in hafte,
That through their pride have broke their necks
(at laft

354 *On Bibens.*

Bibens to shew his liberality,
Made *Lusus* drunk ; a noble quality,
And much esteem'd, which *Bibens* fain would
To be the signe of his familiar-love.   (prove,
Lusus beware, thou'lt finde him in the end,
Familiar devill, no familiar friend.

355 *On Tobacco.*

Things which are common, common men do
The better sort do common things refuse: (use,
Yet countrys-cloth-breech,& court-velvet-hose,
Puff both alike, Tobacco, through the nose.

356 *In Superbum.*

Rustick *Superbus* fine new cloath's hath got,
Of Taffata and Velvet, fair in sight;
The shew of which hath so bewitch'd the sot,
That he thinks Gentleman to be his right.
   But he's deceiv'd ; for, true that is of old,
   An Ape's an Ape, though he wear cloth of
                              (gold.

I   357 *On*

357 *On Infidus.*

Infidus was fo free of oathes laft day,   (fay:
That he would fwear, what e're he thought to
But now fuch is his chance,whereat he's griev'd,
The more he fwears, the leffe he is believ'd.

358 *On Chriftmas-Ivy.*

At *Chriftmas* men do alwaies Ivie get,
And in each corner of the houfe it fet.
But why do they, then, ufe that *Bacchus* weed?
Becaufe they mean, then, *Bacchus*-like to feed.

359 *On Bacchus.*

Pot-lifting-*Bacchus*, to the earth did bend
His k ee, to drink a Health unto his friend :
And there he did, fo long, in liquor pour,
That he lay quite fick-drunk upon the floor.
Judge,was not there a drunkards kindnes fhown,
To drink his friend a Health, and lofe his own?

360 *Of a fat man.*

He's rich,that hath great in-comes by the year;
Then that great belly'd man is rich, Ile fwear :
                   For

For sure, his belly ne'r so big had bin,
Had he not daily had great comings-in.

361 *Vindicta vim sequitur.*

Kitt being kick'd and spurr'd, pursues the Law,
That doom'd the dammage at twice forty pence.
Wch, whē the party wch had wrong'd him, saw,
Thought 'twas too great a fine for such offence.
 Why then, quoth *Kitt,* if I too much request,
 Thou maist at any time kick out the rest.

363 *On Flaccus.*

Flaccus being yong, they said he was a Gull;
Of his simplicity, each mouth was full :
And pitying him, they'd say, the foolish Lad
Would be deceived, sure, of all he had.
His youth is past, now may they turn him loose;
For why? the Gull is grown to be a Goose.

36 *Per plumas anser.*

See how yong *Rufus* walks in green each day,
As if he ne'r was youthfull untill now : (gray,
E're Christmas next, his green Goose will be
And those high burnish'd plumes in's cap will
       (bow.

✚✚✚✚✚✚✚✚✚✚✚✚✚✚✚✚✚✚✚✚✚✚✚✚

But you do wrong him, since his purse is full
To call him Goose, that is so yong a Gull.

364 *Of Ienkyn.*

Ienkyn is a rude clown, go tell him so.
What need I tell, what he himfelf doth know
Perhaps he doth not, then he is a fot;
For tell me, what knows he that knows it not

365 *To Fortune.*

Poets fay Fortune's blinde, and cannot fee,
And therefore to be born withall, if fhe
Sometimes drop gifts on undeferving wights:
But fure they are deceiv'd; fhe hath her fight,
    Els could it not at all times fo fall out, (out
    That fools fhould have, & wife men go with

366 *Vnde venis memora.*

With earthen plate, *Agathocles*, they fay,
Did ufe to meal; fo ferv'd with *Samo's* clay,
When jewell'd plate, and rugged earth was by,
He feem'd to mingle wealth and poverty.
One ask'd the caufe: he anfwers, I that am
Sicilia's King, from a poor Potter came.
                                        Hence

Hence learn, thou that art rais'd from mean
To ludden riches, to be temperate.   (eltate,

367 *On Leucus.*

Leucus loves life, yet liveth wickedly;
He hateth death, yet wisheth he may dy
Honeltly and well: so what is naught he loves,
And what he would have good, he nought ap-
                                    (proves.

368 *On Bifcus.*

I pray you Sir, give *Bifcus* leave to speak,
The Gander loves to hear himself to creak.

369 *In Thrafonem.*

Since *Thrafo* met one stoutly in the field,
He crakes his spirit, & knows not how to yield;
Looks big, swears, strouts with set-side-arms the
Yet gently yields the wal to al he meets.(streets,
And to his friends that asks the reason, why?
His anlwer's this, My self I grace thereby:
For every one the common proverb knows,
That alwaies to the wall the weakeft go's.

I 3   370 *In*

370 *In Cornutum.*

One told his wife,a Hart's-head he had bough
To hang his Hat upon, and home it brought.
To whom his frugal wife,What needs that can
I hope,sweet-heart,your head your hat can bear

371 *On More-dew.*

More-dew the Mercer, with a kinde salute,
Would needs intreat my custom: for a suit:
Here Sir, quoth he, for Sattins, Velvets call,
What e're you please,Ile take your word for a
I thank'd, took, gave my word; say than,
Am I at all indebted to this man ?

372 *On Sims mariage.*

Six moneths, quoth *Sim,* a Suitor, and not sped
I in a sev'n-night did both woo & wed. (shake
Who green fruit loves, must take long pains to
Thine was some downfall,I dare undertake.

373 *On a Wittall.*

I know my fate, and that must bear;
And since I know, I need not fear.

374 *O*

374 On Mopsus.

Mopsus almost, what e're he means to speak,
Before it sir-reverence the way must break :
Such maners hath sir-reverence learnt at school,
That now sir-reverence Mopsus is a fool.

375 On Clym.

Clym cals his wife,& reck'ning all his neighbors,
Just half of them are Cuckolds, he averrs.
Nay fie,quoth she,I would they heard you speak;
You of your self, it seems, no reckoning make.

376 Turpe lucrum Veneris.

Will in a wilfull humour, needs would wed
A wench of wonder,but without a stock;(spred,
Whose fame no sooner through the street was
But thither straight our chiefest Gallants flock.
  Put case she's poor,brings she not chapmen on?
  I hope his stock may serve to graff upon.

377 On Womens faults.

Wee Men in many faults abound,
But two in Women can be found :

The

The worft that from their fex proceeds,
Is naught in words, and naught in deeds.

378 *Si hodie tibi, cras mihi.*

A fcornfull Dame, invited over-night,
To come and dine next morrow with a Knight,
Refus'd his fudden bidding with difdain.
To whom this meffage was return'd again;
Sith with fo fhort time fhe could not difpence,
To pray her come at that day Twelve-moneth
(hence.

379 *On Law.*

Our Civill-Law doth feem a Royall thing,
It hath more Titles than the Spanifh King:
But yet the Common-Law quite puts it down,
In getting, like the Pope, fo many a Crown.

380 *Better loft than found.*

Lo here's a Coyner, yet he fears no death,
For he ne'r ftamps in mettall, but in breath:
Swears from Believe me, & Good-faith & troth,
Up to God-damn-me; and without an oath

Protefts

Protests in nothing, be he ne'r so bare,
He's brave in this, that ne can bravely swear.

381 *In Coam.*

A nor Ω will *Coa* espy,
Till she ascend up the corner'd π.

382 *De Ore.*

Os of O, a Mouth, *Scaliger* doth make;
And from this letter, Mouth his name doth take.
I had been in *Scaligers* belief,
But that I look'd in O, and saw no Teeth.

383 *In Hugonem.*

Though praise, & please, doth *Hugo* never none,
Yet praise, and please, doth *Hugo* ever one;
For praise, and please, doth *Hugo* himself alone.

384 *Fronti nulla fides.*

Cantus that Wooll-ward went, was wondred at;
Which he excus'd, as done through pure contri-
But who so simple, *Cantus*, credits that? (tion.
Tis too wel known, thou art of worse condition.
                                             And

❖❖❖❖❖❖❖❖❖❖❖❖❖❖❖❖❖❖❖❖❖❖❖❖❖❖❖❖

And therefore if no linnen thee begirt,
The naked truth will prove, thou haſt no ſhirt.

385 *On Severus.*

Severus is extreme in Eloquence,
For he creates rare phraſe, but rarer ſence ;
Unto his Serving-man, *alias*, his Boy,
H: utters ſpeech exceeding quaint and coy;
Diminitive, and my defective ſlave ;
My Pleaſures pleaſure is, that I muſt have
My Corps Coverture, and immediately,
T'inſconce my perſon from frigidity.
His man believes all's Welſh his maſter ſpoke,
Till he rails Engliſh, Rogue, go fetch my Cloak.

386 *On a Gallant.*

　　　　　　　　　　　(mine ears?
What Gallant's that, whoſe oathes fly through
How like a Lord of *Pluto's* Court he ſwears !
How Dutch-man. like he ſwallows down his
How ſweet he takes Tobacco, til he ſtink! (drink!
How lofty ſprighted, he diſdains a Boor ;
How faithfull hearted he is to a ——— !
How cock-tail proud he do h himſelf advance !
How rare his Spurs do ring the Morrice-dance,
　　　　　　　　　　　　　　　　Now

Now I protest, by Mistris *Susans* Fann,
He and his Boy will make a proper Man.

387 *Against Caius.*

Twenty small pieces I'd have borrowed late,
Which, if bestow'd, had been a gift not great :
For, 'twas a rich friend whom I ask'd, and old;
Whose crowded chests would scarce his riches
   (hold.
He cry's, Turn Lawyer, and thou'lt thrive : I'd
   (have
No Conncell, *Caius*, give me what I crave.

388 *On* Vertue, Milla's *maid.*

Saith *Aristotle, Vertue* ought to be
Communicative of her self, and free ;
And hath not *Vertue, Milla's* maid, been so ?
Who's grown hereby, as big as she can go.

389 *On Corydon.*

An home-spun Peasant with his Urine-glasse,
The Doctour ask'd what Country-man he was.
Quoth *Corydon*, with making legs full low,
Your Worship , that, shall by my Water know.
           390 *Fami*

389 *Fama mendax.*

Report , thou sometime art ambitious,
At other times, too sparing, covetous;
But many times exceeding envious,
And out of time most dev'lish, furious.
  Of some,or all of these,I dare compound thee;
  But for a Lyer ever have I found thee.

390 *On a Spanish souldier.*

A Spanish souldier, sick unto the death,
His Pistoll to's Physician did bequeath.
Who did demand, what should the reason be,
'Bove other things to give him that.(Quoth he)
This, with your practise joyned,you may kill,
Sir, all alive, and have the world at will.

391 *On Otho.*

Three daughters *Otho* hath, his onely heirs,
But will by no means let them learn to write;
'Cause, after his own humour, much he fears,
They'l one day learn, Love-letters to indite.
  The yongest now's with childe;who taught her
  Or of her self learn'd she to hold her pen?(then,

392 *On*

392 *On Hypocrisy.*

As Venison in a poor mans kitchin's rare,
So Hypocrites and Usurers in Heaven are.

393 *On Man and Woman.*

When Man and Woman dies, as Poets sung,
His Heart's the last that stirs, of hers, the Tongue.

394 *On Fabullus.*

I ask'd *Fabullus*, why he had no wife?
(Quoth he) because I'd live a quiet life.

395 *On Furnus.*

Furnus takes pains, he need not without doubt;
O yes, he labours much. How? with the Gowt.

396 *On a Thief.*

A Thief condemned for a hainous crime,
Was for to lose his Tongue at the same time:
But he the Court intreats with feigned tears,
To spare his Tongue, and cut off both his Ears.

To

To t is, the Judge, and all the Bench agreed,
A d for th'Executioner sent with speed:
Who being com ,and searching,there was found
No Ears,but Hairs; at which,all laughed round.
Saith th'Judge,thou haft no Ears, Sir (quoth the
    (wight)
Where there is nought , the King must lose his
    (right.

397 *Quid n m ebrietas ?*

Ruhin reports, his Miſtris is a Punk; .
Which being told Her, was no whit diſmaid,
For ſure as death (quoth ſhe)the villains drunk,
And in that taking, knows not what he ſaid.
  'Twas well excus'd, but oft it comes to paſſe,
  That true we finde, *In vino veritas.*

398 *Infirmis-animoſus.*

Pontus by no means from his coyn departs,
Z'foot, will you have of men more than their
    (hearts?

399 *A culina ad curiam.*

Lixa, that long a Serving-groom hath been,
Will now no more the man be known or ſeen:
And reaſon good, he hath that place reſign'd,
Witnes his cloak,throughout with velvet lin'd.
            Which

Which by a Paradox comes thus to paſſe,
The greaſie Gull is turn'd a gallant aſſe.

400 *Fruſtra vocaveris keri.*

Dick had but two words to maintain him ever,
And tl at was, Stand; and after, ſtand-Deliver.
But *Dick's* in Newgate, and he fears ſhall never
Be bleſt again with that ſweet word, Deliver.

401 *Magnis non eſt morandum.*

See how *Silenus* walks accompliſhed,
With due performance of his fathers Page:
Looks back of purpoſe to be honoured,
And on each ſlight occaſion 'gins to rage;
  You villain, dog, where hath your ſtay bin ſuch?
  Quoth he, the Broaker would not lend ſo much.

402 *Puduit ſua damna referre.*

Such ill ſucceſſe had *Dick,* at Dice, laſt night,
As he was forc'd, next day, play leaſt in ſight:
But if you love him, make thereof no ſpeeches,
He loſt his Rapier, Cloak, and velvet Breeches.

403 Ni-

403 *Nimis-docuit consuetudo.*

Old *Fucus* board is oft replenished,
But nought thereof must be diminished,
Vnless some worthless upper-dish or twain;
The rest for service still again remain.
His man that us'd to bring them in for show,
Leaving a dish upon the bench below,
Was by his Master (much offended) blam'd:
Which he, as brief, with answer quickly fram'd;
'Tath been so often brought afore this day,
As now ch'ad thoft it self had known the
(way.

404 *Poculo junguntur amici.*

A health, saith *Lucas*, to his Loves bright eye;
Which not to pledge, were much indignity:
You cannot do him greater courtesie,
Than to be drunk, and damn'd for company.

405 *Nullum stimulum ignavis.*

Cæcus awake, was told the Sun appear'd,
Which had the darkness of the morning clear'd
But *Cæcus* sluggish, thereto makes reply,
The Sun hath further far to go than I.

406 *Detur laus digniori.*

Miſtris *Marina* 'mongſt ſome goſſipsſate,
Where faces were the Subject of their chat ;
Some look'd too pale, ſome ſeem'd too fiery red,
Some brown, ſome black, and ſome ill faſhioned.
Good Lord (quoth ſhe) you all are much to blame,
Let's alone, and praiſe the maker of the ſame :
Her Chamber maid, who heard her, ſtanding by,
Said, then love me, for that you know was I.

407 *Non penna, ſed uſus.*

Caius accounts himſelfe accurſt of men,
Only becauſe his Lady loves him not :
Who, till he taught her, could not hold her Pen,
And yet hath ſince, another Tutor got.
   Caius, it ſeems, thy skill ſhe did but cheapen,
   And means to try him at another weapen.

408 *An abſolute Gallant.*

If you will ſee true valour here diſplay'd,
Heare *Poly-phemus,* and be not afraid :
D'ye ſee me wrong'd, and will ye thus reſtrain me ?
Sir let me go, for by theſe hilts I'le braine ye.
                    K   Shall

✥✥✥✥✥✥✥✥✥✥✥✥✥✥✥✥✥✥✥✥✥✥✥✥✥

Shall a bafe patch,with appearance wrong me ?
I'le kill the villaine, pray do not prolong me ;
Call my Tobacco putrified ftuffe ?
Tell me it ftinks ? fay it is droffe I fnuffe ?
Sirrah what are you ? why fir what would you ?
I am a Prentice, and will knock you too :
O are you fo ? I cry you mercy then,
I am to fight with none but Gentlemen.

409   *In Dolentem.*

Dolens doth fhew his purfe, and tels you this,
It is more horrid than a Peft-houfe is ;
For in a Peft-houfe many mortals enter,
But in his purfe one angell dares not venture.

410   *Ambo-dexter.*

Two Gentlemen of hot and fiery fp'rite,
Took boat and went up weft-ward to go fight ;
Embarked both, for Wend-worth they fet Sail,
And there arriving with a happy gale.
The Water-men difcharged for their fare,
Then to be parted, thus their minds declare :
Pray Oares, fay they, ftay here, and come not nigh,
We go to fight a little,but here by :

The

The Water-men, with Staves did follow then,
And cry'd, oh hold your hands, good Gentlemen,
You know the danger of the Law, forbear;
So they put weapons up, and fell to swear.

411 *On a Gallant.*

Sirrah come hither, boy, take view of me,
My Lady I am purpos'd to go see;
What, doth my Feather flourish with a grace?
And this my curled hair become my face?
How decent doth my doublet's forme appear?
I would I had my sute in Hounds-ditch here.
Do not my Spurs pronounce a silver sound?
Is not my hose-circumference profound?
Sir these be well, but there is one thing ill,
Your Taylor with a sheet of paper-bill,
Vow's he'll be paid, and Sergeants he hath fee'd,
Which wait your comming forth to do the deed.
Boy God-a-mercy, let my Lady stay,
I'le see no Counter for her sake to day.

412 *In sextum.*

Sextus sixe pockets wears; two for his uses,
The other four, to pocket up abuses.

✦✦✦✦✦✦✦✦✦✦✦✦✦✦✦✦✦✦✦✦✦✦✦✦

413 *Tom's Fortune.*

Tom tels he's robb'd, and counting all his losses,
Concludes, all's gone, the world is full of crosses:
If all be gone, *Tom* take this comfort then,
Th'art certain never to have crosse agen.

414 *Opus & Usus.*

Opus for need, consum'd his wealth apace,
And ne're would ceafe untill he was undone;
His brother *Usus* liv'd in better cafe
Than *Opus* did, although the eldest Son.
    'Tis strange it should be so, yet here was it,
Opus had all the Land, *Usus* the Wit.

415 *A good Wife.*

A Batchelor would have a Wife were wife,
Faire, rich, and yong, a maiden for his bed—
Nor proud, not churlish, but of faultlesse fife;
A Country hufwife, in the City bred.
    But he's a fool, and long in vain hath staid;
He should befpeak her, there's none ready made.

416 *On an inconstant Mistris.*

I dare not much say, when I thee commend,
Lest thou be changed e're my prayses end.

417 *In Lesbiam.*

Why should I love thee *Lesbia*? I no reason see,
Then out of reason, *Lesbia* I love thee.

418 *In Paulinum.*

Paul by day wrongs me, yet he daily swears.
He wisheth me as well as to his soul:
I know his drift to damne that he nought cares,
To please his body; therefore good friend *Paul*,
  If thy kind Nature, will affoord me grace,
  Hereafter love me in thy body's place.

419 *On Zeno.*

Zeno would faine th'old widow *Egle* have;
Trust me she's wise, for she is rich and brave:
But *Zeno*, *Zeno*, she will none of you,
In my mind she's the wiser of the two.

R 3   420 *To*

420 *To Cotta.*

Be not wroth *Cotta*, that I not falute thee,
I uf'd it whilft I wor thy did repute thee ;
Now thou art made a painted faint, and I,
Cotta, will not commit Idolatry.

421 *To Women.*

Ye that have beauty, anu withall no pity,
Are like a prick-fong leffon without ditty.

422 *On Creta.*

Creta doth love her husband wondrous well,
It needs no proof, for every one can tell :
So ftrong's her love, that if I not miftake,
It doth extend to others, for his fake.

423 *On Prifcus.*

Why ftill doth *Prifcus* ftrive to have the wall?
Becaufe he's often drnnk, and fears to fall.

424 *Idi*

424. *Ictus piscator sapit.*

Brutus at length escap'd the Surgeons hands,
Begins to frollique as if all were well ;
And would not for the worth of thrice his lands,
Endure the brunt of such another hell ;
   But leaves this farewell, for his Physicks hire ;
   The child that's burnt, for ever dreads the fire.

425 *On Rufus.*

At all, quoth *Rufus*, set ye, what you dare ?
I'le throw at all, and 'twere a peck of gold ;
No life lies on't, then coyn I'le never spare,
Why *Rufus*, that's the cause of all that's sold.
   For with franck gamesters it doth oft befall,
   They throw at all, till thrown quite out of all.

426 *On Tobacco.*

Tobacco is a weed of so great power,
That it (like earth) doth all it feeds, devour.

K 4   427 *Nec*

✤✤ ✤✤✤✤✤✤✤✤✤✤✤✤ ✤✤✤✤✤✤✤✤✤✤✤

427 *Nec vultus indicat virum.*

Dick in a raging deep difcourtefie,
Call'd an Attorny meer neceffity :
The more Knaue he, admit he had no Law,
Muft he be flouted at by every Daw ?

428. *On Furius.*

Furius a Lover was, and had loving fits,
He lov'd fo madly, that he loft his wits ;
Yet he loft nought, yet grant I he was mad,
How could he loofe that which he never had ?

429 *Fooles Fortune.*

God fends fools Fortune, but not to all,
For fome are great fools, whofe fortunes are fmall.

430 *Tace fed age.*

Little or nothing faid, foon mended is,
But they that nothing do, do moft amiffe.

431 *On a Mad man.*

One ask'd a mad-man if a wife he had ?
A wife, quoth he, I never was so mad.

432 *To Scilla.*

If it be true, that promise is a debt,
Then *Scilla* will her freedome hardly get ;
For if she hath vow'd her service to so many,
She'll neither pay them all, nor part from any.
Yet she to satisfy her debts, desires
To yeild her body (as the Law requires.)

433 *Nescis, quid serus vesper vehat.*

Lyncus deviseth as he lies in bed,
What new apparrell, he were best to make him :
So many fashions flow within his head,
As much he fears the Taylor will mistake him :
   But he mistook him not, that by the way,
   Did for his old suit lay him up, that day.

434 *To Ficus.*

Ficus hath lost his nose, but knows not how,
And that seems strange to every one that knows it :
                 Me-

Methinks I fee it written in his brow,
How,wherefore, and the caufe that he did loofe it.
  To tell you true, *Ficus* I thus fuppofe,
   'Twas fome French Caniball, bit off your nofe.

435   *Of Arnaldo.*

Arnaldo free from faulc, demands his wife,
Why he is burthen'd with her wicked life?
Quoth fhe, good husband, do not now repent,
I far more burthens bear,yet am content.

436   *Quis nifi mentis inops—*

Ware profer'd, ftinks, yet ftay good Proverb, ftay,
Thou art deceiv'd, as clients beft can fay;
Who profering trebble fees, for fingle care,
It's well accepted, gold it is fuch ware.

437   *On a Friend indeed.*

A reall friend a Canon cannot batter;
With nom'nall friends, a Squib's a perilous matter.

438 *Mans*

438   *Mans ingreſſe, and egreſſe.*

Nature, which headlong, into life did throng us,
With our feet forward, to our grave doth bringus :
What is leſſe ours, than this our borrowed breath ?
We ſtumble into life, we go to death.

439   *On bad debtors.*

Bad debtors are good lyers ; for they ſay,
I'le pay you without fail, on ſuch a day :
Come is the day, to come the debt is ſtill,
So ſtill they lye, though ſtand in debt they will.
But *Fulcus* hath ſo oft ly'd in this wiſe,
That now he lies in Lud-gate for his lyes.

440   *On a fooliſh dolt.*

A Juſtice walking o're the frozen Thames,
The Ice about him round, began to crack ;
He ſaid to's man, here is ſome danger, *James,*
I prethee help me over on thy back.

441   *On Panurgus.*

Panurgus pryes in high and low affairs,
He talks of forraigne, and our civill ſtate :

                                   But

But for his own, he neither counts nor cares;
That he refers to fortune and his fate,
 His neighbors faults ftraight in his face he'l find,
 But in a bag he laps his own behind.

442 *To a ſleeping talker.*

In ſleep thou talk'ſt unfore-thought myſteries,
And utter'ſt unfore-feen things, with cloſe eyes:
How wel wouldſt thou diſcourſe, if thou wert dead,
Since ſleep, death's image, ſuch fine talk hath bred?

443 *Omne ſimile non eſt idem.*

Together as we walk'd, a friend of mine,
Miſtook a painted Madam for a ſigne
That in a window ſtood; but I acquainted,
Told him it was no woodden ſigne was painted,
But Madam——yea true ſaid he,
Yet 'tis little ſigne of modeſty.

444 *Qui ebrius laudat temperantiam.*

Severus likes not theſe unſeaſon'd lines,
Of rude abſurdities, times foul abuſe,
To all poſterities, and their aſſignes,
That might have bin, ſaith he, to better uſe.

What

What fencelesse gull, but reason may convince,
Or jade so dull, but being kick'd will wince.

445 *On Misus.*

They say the Usurer *Misus* hath a mill,
Which men to powder grindeth cruelly ;
But what is that to me ? I feare no ill,
For smaller than I am, I cannot be.

446 *On wisdome and vertue.*

Wise-men are wiser than good-men, what then ?
'Tis better to be wiser than wise men.

447 *On Ducus.*

Ducus keeps house, and it with reason stands,
That he keep house, hath sold away his lands.

448 *On Mysus, and Mopsus.*

Mysus and *Mopsa* hardly could agree,
Striving about superiority :
The Text which saith that man and wife are one,
Was the chief argument they stood upon.

She

She held, they both one woman should become:
He held,they should be man, and both but one.
So they contended dayly, but the strife ;
Could not be ended, till both were one wife.

448   *On Photinus.*

I met *Photynus* at the B. Court,
Cited (as he said) by a knave relator :
I ask'd him wherefore? he in laughing sort,
Told me it was but for a childish matter.
    How ere he laught it out,he lied not :
    Indeed'twas childish, for the child he got.

449   *On Castriotes.*

See, see, what love is now betwixt each fist,
Since *Castriotes* had a scabby wrist :
How kindly they, by clawing one another,
As if the left hand were the right hands brother.

450   *New Rhetoricke.*

Good arguments without coyn,will not stick
To pay, and not to say's best Rhetorick.

451 Ett

451   *Est mibi Diva parens.*

Owinus wondreth, since he came from Wales,
What the description of this Isle might be ;
That ne're had seen but mountains, hils, and dales,
Yet would he boast, and stand on's pedegree.
  From Rice ap *Richard*, sprung from *Dick a Cow*,
  Be cod was right good gentle-man, look ye now?

452   *On Thirsites.*

Although *Thirsites* have a filthy facae,
And staring eyes, and little outward grace :
Yet this he hath, to make amends for all,
Nature her selfe, is not more naturall.

453   *On Zoylus.*

If Souldiers may obtain four Termes of war,
Muskets should be the pleaders, Pikes the bar :
For black bags, Bandeleirs, Jackets for gownes,
Angels for fees ; we'll take no more crack't crowns.

454   *On a swearing Gallant.*

What God cõmands, this wretched creature loathes,
He never names his Maker, but by oathes :
                                    And

And weares his tongue of such a damned fashion,
That swearing is his only recreation.
In morning, even assoon as he doth rise,
He swears his sleep is scarcely out of 's eyes;
Then makes him ready, swearing all the while,
The drowzy weather did him much beguile.
Got ready, he, to dice or tables goes,
Swearing an oath, at every cast he throws:
To dinner next, and then in stead of Grace,
He swears his stomack is in hungry case.
No sooner din'd, but calls, come take away,
And swears 'tis late, he must goe see a Play.
There sits, and swears, to all he hears and see's,
This speech is good, that action disagrees.
So takes his Oares, and swears he must make hast,
His houre of Supper-time is almost past.

455 *On a long Beard.*

Thy Beard is long, better it would thee fit,
To have a shorter Beard, and longer wit.

456 *On my Selfe.*

Who seeks to please all men each way,
And not himselfe offend;

H

He may begin to work to day,
But God knows when hee'l end.

457 *To the mis-interperter.*

                        (mince,
Cease gaul'd backt guilt, those inscious lines to
The world wil know y'are rubd if once you wince
They hem within their seeming Critique wall,
Particularly none, generally all :
'Mongst which if you have chanc'd to catch a prick
Cry wo-hy if you will, but do not kick.

458 *On a Mother and her son having but two eyes betwixt them, each one.*

A half blind-boy, born of a half blind mother,
Peerlesse for beauty, save compas'd to th' other;
Faire boy, give her thine eye and she will prove
The Queen of beauty, thou the God of love.

459 *To his quill.*

Thou hast been wanton, therefore it is meet,
Thou shouldst do penance do it in a sheet.

L   460

460 *Of Chirst crucified.*

When red the Sun goes down, we ufe to fay
It is a figne, we fhall have a faire day :   (hence
Blood red the Sun of Heaven went down from
And we have had faire weather ever fince.

461 *On himfelfe.*

Mirth pleafeth fome, to others 'tis offence,
Some comend plain conceits,fome profound fence
Some wifh a witty jeft, fome diflike that,   (what
And moft would have themfelves they know not
Then he that would pleafe all,and himfelfe too,
Takes more in hand than he is like to doe.

462 *To young men.*

Yong men fly, when beauty darts
Amorous glances at your hearts,
The fixt marke gives your fhooter aime,
And Ladyes lookes have power to maime,
Now 'twixt their lips,now in their eyes
Wrapt in a kiffe or fmile love lyes,
Then fly betimes for onely they
Conquer love that run away.

463 *The pens profopopeia to
the Scrivener.*

Thinke who when you cut the quill,
Wounded was yet did no ill;
When you mend me, thinke you muſt
Mend your ſelfe, elſe you're unjuſt
When you dip my nib in Inke,
Thinke on him that gall did drinke,
When the Inke ſheds from your pen,
Thinke who ſhed his blood for men;
When you write, but thinke on this,
And you ne're ſhall write amiſſe.

464 *A raritie.*

If thou bee'ſt born to ſtrange ſights,
Things inviſible to ſe:
Ride ten thouſand dayes and nights,
Till age ſnow white haires on thee.
  And thou when thou return'ſt wilt tell me;
  All ſtrange wonders that befell thee,
And thou 'lt ſweare that no where
Lives a maiden true and faire.

465 *Vpon Tom Toltham's nose.*

The radiant colour of *Tom Toltham's* nose,
Puts down the lilly and obscures the rose ;
Had I a jewell of such pretious hew ,
I would present it to some Monarch's view ,
No subject should possesse such jems as those
Ergo, the King must have *Tom Toltham's* nose.

466 *Vpon Thorough-good an vnthrift.*

Thy sir name *Thorough-good* besitteth thee,
Thou *Thorough-good,* and good goes thorough thee
Nor thou in good,nor good in thee doth stay ,
Both of you, thorough goe, and passe away.

467 *In Amorem.*

Love, if a God thou art, then evermore thou must
    Be mercifull and just ,
If just thou be, O wherefore doth thy dart ,
Wound mine alone, and not my Mistrisse heart?
If mercifull, then why am I to paine reserv'd,
    Who have thee truly serv'd ?
Whiles she that for thy power cares not a fly,
Laughs thee to scorn, and lives at liberty :
                    Then

Then if a God thou wilt accounted be
Heale me like her, or elſe wound her like me.

468 *A riddle on a pound of candles.*

One evening as cold as cold might bee,
With froſt and ſnow, and pinching weather,
Companions about three times three,
Lay cloſe all in a bed together;
  Yet one after other they tooke a heat,
  And dy'd that night all in a ſweat.

469 *On the new dreſſings.*

Ladyes that weare black cypreſſe vailes,
Turn'd lately to white linnen railes,
And to your girdle weare your bands,
And ſhew your armes in ſtead of hands:
What can you do in Lent more meet,
As fitteſt dreſſe, than weare a ſheet:
Twas once a band, tis now a cloake,
An acorne one day proves an oake,
Weare but your lawn unto your feet,
And then your band will prove a ſheet:

By

✦✦✦✦✦✦✦✦✦✦✦✦✦✦✦✦✦✦✦✦✦✦✦✦✦✦✦✦✦✦✦✦✦✦✦

By which device and wife exceſſe,
You do your pennance in a dreſſe,
And none ſhall know, by what they ſee,
Which Lady's cenſur'd, which goes free.

469 *Thus anſwered.*

Blacke Cypreſſe vailes are ſhrouds of night,
White linnen railes are railes of light;
Which though we to our girdles weare,
W'have hands to keepe your armes off there;
Who makes our bands to be a cloake,
Makes *John* a *Stiles* of *John* an *Oke*:
We weare our linnen to our feet,
Yet need not make our band a ſheet.
Your Clergie wears as long as wee,
Yet that implyes conformitie:
Be wiſe, recant what you have writ,
Leaſt you do pennance for your wit:
Love charmes have power to weave a ſtring
Shall tye you, as you ty'd your ring,
Thus by loves ſharpe, but juſt decree
You may be cenſur'd, we go free.

470 *Amicitia.*

What's friendſhip? 'tis a treaſure,
       'tis a pleaſure: Bred

✠✠✠✠✠✠✠✠✠✠✠✠✠✠✠✠✠✠✠✠✠✠✠

Bred 'twixt two worthy ſpirits,
       by their merits :
'Tis two minds in one, meeting
       never fleeting :
Two wils in one conſenting ,
       each contenting,
One breſt in two divided, yet not parted ;
A double body, and yet ſingle hearted ;
Two bodies making one, through ſelf election ,
Two minds, yet having both but one affection.

471. *To his Miſtriſſe.*

I cannot pray you in a ſtudied ſtile ,
Nor ſpeak words diſtant from my heart a mile ;
I cannot viſit Hide-parke every day ,
And with a hackney court my time away ;
I cannot ſpanniolize it weeke by week ,
Or waite a moneth to kiſſe your hand or cheek ;
If when you'r lov'd you cannot love againe,
Why doe but ſay ſo, I am out of paine.

472 *On the Queene of Bohemia.*

You meaner Beauties of the night ,
Which poorely ſatisfie our eyes;

More

More by your number then your light;
The common people of the skies:
    What are ye when the moon shall rise?
You violets that first appeare,
By your purple mantle known;
Like proud virgins of the yeere,
As if the Spring were all your own;
    What are you when the rose is blown?
You wandring chaunters of the wood,
That fill the ayre with natures layes:
Thinking your passions underftood,
By weak accents, where's your praise,
    When *Philomell* her voyce shall raise:
So when my Princeffe shall be seen,
In sweetnes of her lookes and mind:
By vertues first, then choyce a Queen,
Tell me, was she not defign'd,
    Th' eclipse and glory of her kind?

473 *To his noble friend.*

There's no neceffity that can exclude
The pooreft being from a gratitude;
For when the ftrength of fortune lends no more,
He that is truely thankefull is not poore,

                                        Yours

Yours be the bounty then, mine the great debt,
On which no time, nor power can ranſome ſet.

474 *Fatum Supremum.*

All buildings are but monuments of death,
All clothes but winding ſheets for our laſt knell,
All dainty fattings for the worms beneath,
All curious muſique, but our paſſing bell;
   Thus death is nobly waited on, for why?
   All that we have is but deaths livery.

475 *On his Mrs. death*

Unjuſtly we complain of fate,
  For ſhort'ning our unhappy dayes,
When death doth nothing but tranſlate
  And print us in a better phraſe;
Yet who can chooſe but weep? not I,
  That beautie of ſuch excellence,
And more vertue then could dy;
  By deaths rude hand is raviſh'd hence,
Sleepe bleſt creature in thine Urne,
  My ſighes, my teares ſhall not awake thee,
I but ſtay untill my turne
  And then, Oh then! I'le overtake thee.

476 *Æque facilitas ae difficultas nocet amoru.*

I love not her that at the firſt cries I,
I love not her that doth me ſtill deny,
Be ſhe too hard ſhee'll cauſe me to deſpaire,
Be ſhe too eaſie, ſhee's as light as faire;
'Tis hard to ſay whether moſt hurt procure,
She that is hard or eaſy to allure,
If it be ſo, then lay me by my ſide
The hard, ſoft, willing and unwilling bride.

477 *In monumentá Weſtminſterienſia.*

Mortality behold and feare,
What a change of fleſh is here;
Thinke how many royall bones,
Sleep within this heap of ſtones,
Here they ly, had realmes and lands;
Who now want ſtrength to ſtir their hands;
Where from their Pulpits feel'd with duſt,
They preach, In greatnes is no truſt;
Here's an acre ſown indeed,
With the richeſt royal ſt ſeed,
That the earth did e're ſuck in
Since the firſt man dy'd for ſin,
Here the bones of birth have cry'd,
Though Gods they were, as men they dy'd:
Here

Here are fands, ignoble things,
Drop'd from the ruin'd fides of Kings;
Here's a world of pompe and ftate,
Buried in duft, once dead by fate.

478 *Semel infaluimus.*

Beldam, God bleffe thee, thou want'ft nought but
And having gotten that, we'r freed from it, (wit
Bridewell, I cannot any way difpraife thee
For thou doft feed the poore and jerke the lazie.
New-gate, of thee I cannot much complaine;
For once a moneth, thou freeft men out of paine,
But from the Counters gracious Lord defend us:
To Bedlam, Bridewell, or to Newgate fend us,
For there in time wit, worke, or law fets free;
But here wit, work, nor law gets liberty.

479 *On the Marriage of one Turbolt, with Mrs. Hill.*

What are *Deucalions* dayes return'd that we,
A *Turbolt* fwimming on a *Hill* do fee?
What fhall we in this age fo ftrange report,
That fifhes leave the fea on hils to fport'?
And yet this *hill*, though never tir'd with ftanding
Lay gently down to give a *Turbolt* landing.

480

480 *Upon Annas marriadge with a lawyer.*

Anne is an angell, what if so shee be?
What is a angell? but a lawyers fee.

481 *In Cupidinem.*

Who grafts in blindnes may mistake his stock,
Love hath no tree, but that whose bark is smock.

482 *Ænigma.*

The Devill men say in Devonshire dy'd of late;
But Devonshire lately liv'd in rich estate,
Till Rich his toyes did Devonshire so bewitch,
As Devonshire dy'd and left the Devill rich.

483 *On Cupid.*

Why feign they *Cupid* robbed of sight;
Can he whose seat is in the eye, want light?

484 *An answer.*

Experience shews, and reason doth decree
That he who sits in's owne light cannot see.

✦✦✦✦✦✦✦✦✦✦✦✦✦✦✦✦✦✦✦✦✦✦✦✦✦

485 *Barten Holiday to the Puritan*
on his Technogamia.

'Tis not my perſon, nor my play ,
But my ſirname, *Holiday* ,
That does offend thee, thy complaints
Are not againſt me, but the Saints ;
So ill doſt thou endure my name ,
Becauſe the Church doth like the ſame ,
A name more awfull to the puritane
Then *Talbot* unto france, or *Drake* to Spaine.

486 *On a Picture.*

This face here pictur'd time ſhall longer have ,
Then life the ſubſtance of it, or the grave ,
Yet as I change from this by death I know ,
I ſhall like death, the liker death I grow.

487 *In Meretrices.*

The law hangs theeves for their unlawfull ſtealing,
The law carts bawds for keeping of the doore ,
The law doth puniſh rogues, for roguiſh dealing,
The law whips both the pander and the whore;
But yet I muſe from whence this law is grown ;
Whores muſt not ſteal, yet muſt not uſe their own.

478

✦✦✦✦✦✦✦✦✦✦✦✦✦✦✦✦✦✦✦✦✦✦✦✦✦✦✦✦

487 *On the Citty Venice.*

When in the Adriatick Neptune faw
How Venice ftood, and gave the feas their law.
Boaft thy Tarpeian towers,now *Jove* faid he,
And *Mars* thy wals, if Tiber 'fore the fea
Thou doft prefer, view both the cities ods,
Thou'lt fay that men built Rome,Venice,the gods.

488 *To a Lady that every morning vfed to paint her face.*

Preferve what nature gave you,nought's more
Th n Belgian colour on a Roman face,   (bafe,
Much good time's loft,you reft your faces debtor,
And make it worfe,ftriving to make it better.

489 *On a Cuckold.*

My friend did tax me ferioufly one morne,
That I would weare, yet could not winde a horne
And I reply'd he perfect truth fhould find it,
Many did weare the horn that could not wind it,
Howe're of all that man may weare it beft,
Who makes claime to it as his ancient creft.

490 Upon Marriage.

Marriage as old men note, hath likened bin
Unto a publique feast or common route,
Where thofe that are without, would fain get in,
And thofe that are within would faine get out.

491 Quicquid non nummus.

The mony'd man can fafely faile all feas,
And make his fortune as himfelfe fhall pleafe,
He can wed *Danae*, and command that now
Acrifius felfe that fatall match allow :
He can declaime, chide, cenfure verfes, write,
And do all things better then *Cato* might ;
He knows the Law and rules it, hath and is
Whole *Servius*, and what *Labeo* can poffeffe,
In briefe let rich men wifh what e're they love,
'Twill come, they in a lock'd cheft keep a *Jove*.

492 On Annas a news-monger.

Annas hath long eares for all news to paffe :
His eares muft needs be long for hee's an affe.

493

494 *Semel infanivimus omnes.*

Thus have I waded through a worthleſſe taske,
Whereto I truſt there's no exception ta'ne ,
For meant to none, I anſwer ſuch as aske ,
'Tis like apparell made in birchen lane ;
 If any pleaſe to ſuit themſelves and weare it,
 The blames not mine but theirs that needs will
         weare it.

495 *To Aulus.*

Some (ſpeaking in their own renown)
Say that this book, was not exactly done;
I care not much, like banquets, let my bookes
Rather be pleaſing to the gueſts then cooks.

496 *Ad ſeſquipedales poetaſtros.*

Hence *Braurons* God to *Tauriminion* ,
And you Levaltoring Corybants be gone ;
Fly thundring Bronſterops to Hippocrene,
And *Maures* to nimph nurſing *Mytelene* ;
Griſly *Mægera's* necromantique ſpell
Depart to blacke nights *Acheronticke* cell :
Avaunt transformed *Epidarian* ,
Unto th' Antipod Iſles of Tabraban,

A

Away *Cyllenius* plumy-pinnion'd God,
With thy peace making wand, make charming rod
And all the rest not daring looke upon
Vranus' blood-borne brood, and fell *Typhon*
Chimera's victor great *Bellepheron*;
Thou vanquisher of Spanish *Gerynn*,
Stout *Asdruball* Sicilian Lord of yore,
Thou that destroyd'st the Calidonian bore;
Couragious conqueror of Creetes Minotaure,
Thou pride of *Memeros'* cloudy Semitaure.
Perseus whose marble stone transforming shield;
Enforc'd the whale, *Andromeda* to yeeld,
You *Argonautes* that scour'd *Syndromades*,
And passt the quicke sands of Semplegades,
Helpe *Demogorgon*, King of heaven and earth,
Chaos Lucina at *Litigiums* birth,
The world with child looks for delivery
Of Cannibals or Poetophagie;
A devillish brood, from Ericthonius,
From Iphidemia, Nox, and Erebus,
Chide *Pegasus* for op'ning Helicon,
And Poets damn to Pery-Phlegeton,
Or make this monstrous birth abortive be
Or else I will shake hands with poetrie.

M

✦✦✦✦✦✦✦✦✦✦✦✦✦✦✦✦✦✦✦✦✦✦✦✦✦✦✦

497 *A Serving man.*

One to a Serving man this counsell sent,
To get a Master that's intelligent;
Then if of him no wages he could get,
Yet he would understand he's in his debt.

498 *Two Theeves.*

Two Theeves by night began a lock to pick,
One in the house awake; thus answer'd quick,
Why how now? what a stir you there do keep,
Goe home again, we are not yet asleep.

499 *A Physitian and a Farrier.*

A neate Physitian for a Farrier sends
To dresse his horse, promising him amends.
Nay (quoth the Farrier) amends is made,
For nothing do we take of our own trade.

500 *A poore Peasant.*

A poore man being sent for to the King,
Began to covet much a certaine thing
Before he went : being but an Iron naile,
His friend did aske him what it would availe ?

Quoth

(Quoth he) this is as good as one of steele,
For me to knock now into fortunes wheele.

501 *Three Pages.*

Three Pages on a time together met,
And made a motion, that each one would let
The other know what hee'd desire to be
Having his wish, thereto they did agree.
Quoth one, to be a Melon I would chuse,
For then I'm sure, none would refuse
To kisse my breech although the sent were hot,
And so they'd know whether I were good or not.

502 *A Gentleman and his Phisitian.*

A Gentleman not richest in discretion,
Was alwayes sending for his own phisition.
And on a time he needs would of him know,
What was the cause his pulse did go so slow?
Why (quoth the Doctor) thus it comes to passe,
Must needs go slow, which goes upon an asse.

503 *A Peasant and his wife.*

A Peasant with his wife was almost wilde,
To understand his Daughter was with childe,
And said if to the girle sh'ad taken heed,
Sh'ad not been guilty of so foule a deed.
Husband (said she) I sweare by cock,
  (Welfare a good old token)
The Dev'll him selfe can't keep that lock
  Which every key can open.

504 *G-L-Asse.*

He that loves Glasse without a G,
Leave out L and that is hee.

—Nihil hic nisi carmina desunt.

EPITAPHS.

1. *On a travelling begger.*

HEre lies a Vagrant perſon whom our lawes,
(Of late growne ſtrict)denied paſſage, cauſe
Hee wandred thus, therefore returne he muſt,
From whence at firſt he hither came, to duſt.

2. *On a Maſon.*

So long the Maſon wrought on other's walles,
That his owne houſe of clay to ruine falles :
No wonder ſpitefull death, wrought his annoy,
He us'd to build, and death ſeekes to deſtroy.

3. *On a Dyer.*

Though death the Dyer colour-leſſe hath made,
Yet he dies pale ; and will not leave his trade ;
But being dead, the meanes yet doth not lacke
To die his friends cloth into mourning blacke.
Some ſure foreſaw his death, for they of late
Vs'd to exclaime upon his dying fate.   (been,
And weake, and faint,he ſeem'd oft-times t'have
For to change colours, often he was ſeen ;
Yet there no matter was ſo foule, but he
Would ſet a colour on it handſomlye.
Death him no unexpected ſtroke could give
That learnt to dye, ſince he began to live.
He ſhall yet prove, what he before hath try'd,
And ſhall once more, live after he hath dy'd.

4. *Of a Schoolemaſter.*

The gramer Schoole a long time taught I have,
Yet all my skill could not decline the grave,
But yet I hope it one day will be ſhow'ne
In no caſe ſave the Ablative alone.

5. *On*

5. *On William Shake-speare.*

Renowned Spencer lye a thought more nigh
To learned Chaucer, and rare Beaumont lye
A little neerer Spencer, to make roome   (tombe
For Shake-speare in your threefold, fourefold
To lodge all foure in one bed make a shift
Vntill Doomes day, for hardly will a fifth
Betwixt this day and that by Fates be slaine,
For whom your curtaines may be drawn againe.
If your precedencie in death doe barre
A fourth place in your sacred Sepulchre;
Vnder this sacred marble of thine owne,
Sleepe rare Tragædian Shake-speare! sleep alone.
Thy unmolested peace in an unshared cave
Possesse as Lord, not tenant of thy grave.
That unto us, and others it may bee
Honour hereafter to be laid by thee.

6. *On a youth.*

Now thou hast Heaven for merit, but 'tis strange
Mortality should envie at thy change :
But God thought us unfit, for such as thee,
And made thee consort of eternitye.

A a 2   We

We grieve not then,that thou to heaven art tak
But that thou haft thy friends fo foone forfaken

7. *On Prince Henry.*

I have no veine in verfe, but if I cou'd,
Diftill on every word a pearle I would.   (ere,
Our forrowes pearles drop not from pens ; but
Whilft other's Mufe ? write, mine onely cries.

8. *On a Foot-boy that dyed with overmuch running.*

Bafe tyrant death thus to affaile one tyr'd
Who fcarfe his lateft breath beeing left expir'd;
And being too too cruell thus to ftay
So fwift a courfe,at length ran quite away.
But pretty boy, be fure it was not death
That left behind thy body out of breath :
Thy foule and body running in a race,
'Thy foule held out ; thy body tyr'd apace,
Thy foule gained, and left that lump of clay
To reft it felfe, untill the latter day

9. *On Hobson the Carrier.*

Hobson, (what's out of sight is out of mind)
Is gone, and left his letters here behind.
He that with so much paper us'd to meet;
Is now, alas! content to take one sheet.

10. *Another.*

He that such carriage store, was wont to have,
Is carried now himselfe unto his grave:
O strange! he that in life ne're made but one,
Six Carriers makes, now he is dead and gone.

11. *Another.*

Here Hobson lyes, prest with a heavy loade,
Who now is gone the old and common Roade;
The waggon he so lov'd, so lov'd to ride,
That he was drawing on, whilst that he dy'd.

12. *Another.*

(swaine
Hobson's not dead, but Charles the Northerne
Hath one for him, to draw his lightsome waine.

A a 3

13. On

13. *On a treacherous Warrener.*

Behold here lyes a fcalded pate quite bare,
In catching conits; who loſt many a hare.

14. *On a faire Damoſell.*

(muſt be,
Life is the Road to death, & death Heavens gate
Heaven is the throne of Chriſt, & Chriſt is life to

15. *On a Foot-man.*

This nimble foot-man ran away from death,
And here he reſted being out of breath ;
Here death him overtooke, made him his ſlave,
And ſent him on an errand to his grave.

16. *On Queene Anne, who dyed in March,*
was kept till Aprill, and buried in May.

March with his winds hath ſtrucke a Cedar tall,
And weeping April mournes the Cedar's fall;
And May intēds her month no flow'rs ſhal bring
Since ſhe muſt loſe, the flow'r of all the ſpring.
                                                    Thy

Thy March his winds have caused April show'rs
And yet sad May must lose his flow'r of flow'rs.

17. *Justus Lipsius.*

Some have high mountaines of Parian stone,
And some in brasse carve their inscription,
Some have their tombes of costly marble rear'd;
But in our teares, onely art thou interr'd.

18. *On a child of two yeeres old, being borne and dying in July.*

Here is laid a July-flow'r
With surviving teares bedew'd
Not despayring of that home
When her spring shall be renew'd;
E're she had her Summer seene,
Shee was gather'd, fresh and greene.

29. *Another.*

Like bird of prey,
Death snatcht away,

A a 4   This

++++++++++++++++++++++++++++++

This harmeleffe dove,
Whofe foule fo pure
Is now fecure
In heaven above.

20. *Another.*

That flefh is graffe
It's grace a flower
Reade e're you paffe
Whom wormes devoure

21. *On a Cobler.*

Death at a Coblers doore oft made a ftand,
And alwaies found him on the mending hand;
At laft came death in very foule weather,
And ript the foale, from the upper leather :
Death put a trick upon him, and what was't
The cobler call'd for's awle, death brought his
(Lafte.

22. *On a Lock-fmith.*

A zealous Lock-fmith dy'd of late,
Who by this time's at heaven-gate
The

The reason why he will not knocke
Is, [cause he meanes to picke the locke.

23. *On a Collier.*

Here lies the Collier Jenkin Dashes,
By whom death nothing gain'd he swore,
For living he was dust and ashes :
And being dead, he is no more.

24. *On Dick Pinner.*

Here lyes Dick Pinner, O ungentle death!
Why did'st thou rob Dick Pinner of his breath?
For living, he by scraping of a pin
Made better dust, then thou hast made of him.

25. *On M. Thomas Best.*

With happie stars he sure is blest,
Where s'ere he goes, that still is Best.

26. *On Robyn.*

Round Robyn's gone, & this grave doth inclose
The pudding of his doublet and his hose.

27. *On Proud Tygeras.*

Proud and foolifh, fo it came to paffe,
He liu'd a Tyger, and he dy'd and Affe.

28. *On John Cofferer.*

Here lyes *Iohn Cofferer*, and takes his reft,
Now he hath chang'd a coffer for a cheft.

29. *On blind and deafe Dicke Freeman.*

Here lyes *Dicke Freeman*
That could not heare, nor fee man.

30. *On a Miller.*

Death without warning, was as bold as briefe,
When he kill'd two in one, Miller & Thiefe.

31. *On*

✦✦✦✦✦✦✦✦✦✦✦✦✦✦✦✦✦✦✦✦✦✦✦✦✦.

31. *On a disagreeing couple.*

Hìc jacet ille, qui aeuties & mille :
    Did scold with his wife,
Cùm illo jacet illa ,quæ communis in villâ
    did quittance his life :
His name was *Nicke*, the which was ficke,
    And that very *male*,
Her name was *Nan*, who lou'd weft a man,
    So gentlemen *vare*.

32. *On a Sack-sucker.*

Good reader bleffe thee, be affur'd,
The fpirit of Sack lyes here immur'd:
Who havock'd all he could come by
For Sack, and here quite fack'd doth lye.

33. *On a Lady.*

Here lyes one dead under this marble ftone,
Who when fhe liv'd, lay under more than one.

34. *On*

34. *On a Weftler.*

Death to this Wreftler, gave a fine fall;
That tript up his heeles, and tooke no hold at all.

35. *On John Death.*

Here's Death intterred, that liu'd by bread,
Then all fhould live, now death is dead

36. *On a Scriuener.*

Here to a period, is the Scriuener come;
This is the laft fheet, his full point this tombe.
Of all afperfions I excufe him not,
'Tis knowne he liu'd not, without many a'blot;
Yet he no ill example fhew'd to any,
But rather gave good coppies unto many :
He in good letters alwaies hath beene bred
And hath writ more, then many men have read.
He rulers had as his command by law,   (draw.
And though he could not hang, yet he could
He far more bond men had & made than any,
A dafh alone of his pen ruin'd many.
                                        That

That not without good reason, we might call
He letters great or little Capitall :
Yet is the Scriveners fate as sure as just,
When he hath all done, then he falls to dust.

37. *On a Chandler.*

(hee
How might his dayes end that made weekes ? or
That could make light, here laid in darkenes bee?
Yet since his weekes were spent how could he
But be depriu'd of light & his trade lose.(chose
Yet dead the Chandler is, and sleep's in peace,
No wonder ! long since melted was his greace :
It seemes that he did evill, for daylight
He hated, and did rather wish the night,
Yet came his workes to light, & were like gold
Prou'd in the fire, but could not tryall hold.
His candle had an end, and death's black night
Is an extinguisher of all his light.

38. *On a young gentle-woman.*

Nature in this small volume was about
To perfect what in women was left out ;

Yet

Yet carefull leaſt a peice ſo well begun
Should want preſervatives when ſhe had done :
E're ſhe could finiſh, what ſhe undertooke,
Threw duſt upon it, and ſhut up the booke.

39. *On an Infant.*

The reeling world turn'd poet, made a play,
I came to ſee't, diſlik't it. went my way

40. *On a Lady dying quickly after her husband.*

He firſt deceaſed, ſhe a little try'd
To live without him, liked not, and dy'd.

41. *On a Smith.*

Farewell ſtout Iron-ſide, not all thine art
Could make a ſhield againſt death's envious dart.
Without a fault no man, his life doth paſſe,
For to his vice the Smith addicted was.
He oft, (as choller is encreas't by fire)
Was in a fume, and much enclin'd to ire.
He had ſo long bin us'd to forge, that he

Was

Was with a blacke coale markt for forgery
But he for witnesse needed not to care,   (fayre.
Who but a blacke-smith was, though ne're so
And opertunities he flacked not
That knew to strike, then when the ir'n was hot
As the doore-nailes he made, hee's now as dead,
Hath them, & death him, hath knockt on the head.

42. *On M͏ͬ. Stone.*

Jerusalems curse is not fulfill'd in mee,
For here a stone upon a stone you see.

43. *On a Child.*

Into this world as stranger to an Inne   (beene
This child came guest-wise, where when it had
Awhile and found nought worthy of his stay,
He onely broke his fast & went away.

44. *On a man drown'd in the snow.*

Within a fleece of silent waters drown'd;
Before my death was knowne a grave I found.
                                        The

That which exil'd my life from her sweet home,
For griefe straight froz it selfe into a tombe.
One element my angry fate thought meet
To be my death,grave,tombe,& winding-sheet.
Phœbus himselfe mine Epitaph had writ,
But blotting many e're he thought one fit;
He wrote untill my grave,and tombe were gone,
And twas an Epitaph that I had none;
For every one that passed by that way,
Without a sculpture read that there I lay ;
Here now the second time untomb'd I lye,
And thus much have the best of Destinie :
Corruption from which onely one was free,
Devour'd my grave but did not feede on mee :
My first grave tooke me from the race of men,
My last shall give me backe to life agen.

45. *On Prince Henry.*

In natur's law 'tis a plaine case to dye,
No cunning Lawyer can demurre on that ;
   For cruell death and destiny,
   Serve all men with a Latitat.
So Princely *Henry*; when his case was try'd,
Confefs'd the action, paid the debt,and dy'd.

46. *On*

✚✚✚✚✚✚✚✚✚✚✚✚✚✚✚✚✚✚✚✚✚✚✚✚✚

46. *On M*ʳ. *Strange.*

Here lyes one Strange, no Pagan, Turke, nor Jew
It's strange, but not so strange as it is true.

47. *On a Scholler.*

Forbeare friend t'unclaspe this booke
Onely in the fore-front looke,
For in it have errours bin,
Which made th'authour call it in :
  Yet know this, 't shall have more worth,
  At the second comming forth.

48. *On a young woman.*

The body which within this earth is laid,
Twice sixe weekes knew a wife, a saint, a maid ;
Fair maid, chast wif, pure saint, yet 'tis not strange
She was a woman therefore pleas'd to change :
And now shee's dead, some woman doth remaine
For still she hopes, once to be chang'd againe.

Bb   48. *On*

49. *On Brawne.*

Here Browne the quondam begger lyes,
  Who counted by his tale,
Full sixscore winters in his life;
  Such vertue is in ale.
Ale was his meate, ale was his drinke,
  Ale did him long reprive,
And could he still have drunke his ale,
  He had beene still alive.

50. *On a lyar.*

Good paffenger! here lyes one here,
That living did lie every where.

51. *On a Dyer.*

He lives with God none can deny,
That while he liv'd to th' world did dye.

52. *On a Candle.*

Here lyes (I wot) a little ftat
That did belong to Jupiter,   Which

Which from him Prometheus stole
And with it a fire-coale.
Or this is that I meane to handle,
Here doth lie a farthing-candle
That was lov'd well, having it's light,
But losing that, now bids good-night.

53. *Another.*

Here lyes the chandlers chiefest say
Here lyes the schollers pale-fac'd boy,
Having nought else but skin and bone
Dy'd of a deepe consumption.

54. *On M. R.*

Who soonest dyes lives long enough,
Our life is but a blast or puffe.
I did resist and strive with death
But soone he put me out of breath;
He of my life thought to bereave me
But I did yeeld onely to breathe me.
O're him I shall in triumph sing,
Thy conquest grave, where is thy sting?

A a 2

55. *On*

❖❖❖❖❖❖❖❖❖❖❖❖❖❖❖❖❖❖❖❖❖❖❖❖❖

55. *On an Inne-keeper.*

It is not I that dye,I doe but leave an Inne, (fin;
Where harbour'd was with me all filthy kind of
It is not I that dye, I doe but now begin
Into eternall joy by faith to enter in.   (my kin
Why weepe you then my friends, my parents &
Lament ye whē I lose,but weep not when I win

56. *On Hobson the Carrier.*

Whom seeke ye sirs? Old Hobson? fye upon
Your tardinesse,the carrier is gone.
Why stare you so ? nay you deserve to faile,
Alas here's naught,but his old rotten maile.
He went a good-while since, no question store
Are glad,who vext he would not goe before :
And some are grieu'd hee's gone so soone away,
The Lord knowes why he did no longer stay.
How could he please you all ? I'm sure of this,
He linger'd soundly howsoe're you misse.
But gone he is, nor was he surely well
At his departure as mischance befell,
For he is gone in such unwonted kinde
As ne're before,his goods all left behinde.

57. *On.*

57. *On Bolus.*

If gentlenesse could tame the fates, or wit
Delude them, Bolus had not dyed yet;
But one that death o're rules in judgement sits,
And saies our sins are stronger than our witts.

58. *On Iuggler.*

Death came to see thy trickes and cut in twaine
Thy thread, why did'st not make it whole againe

59. *On a Child.*

A child and dead? alas! how could it come?
Surely thy thread of life was but a thrumme.

60. *On a Clowne.*

Softly tread this earth upon,
For here lyes our Corydon
Who through care to save his sheepe
Watcht too much, oh let him sleepe!

60. *On Queene Anne.*

Thee to invite the great God sent his star,
Whose friends & kinsmen mightie Princes are

For though they run the race of men and dye,
Death ferves but to refine their majefty.
So did the Queen from hence her court remove,
And left the earth to be enthron'd above. (dyes
Thus is fhe chang'd not dead,no good Prince
But like the day-ftar, onely fets to rife.

62. *On Sir Horatio Palavozeene.*

Here lyes Sir Horatio Palavozeene,
Who robb'd the Pope to pay the Queene,
And was a theife. A theife ? thou ly'ft:
For why, he robb'd but Antichrift.   (Babram,
Him death with his beefome fweept from
Into the bofome of old *Abraham* :
But then came Hercules with his club,
And ftruck him downe to Belzebub.

63. *On an onely child.*

Here lyes the fathers hope, the mothers joy,
Though they feeme haplefle,happy was the boy
Who of this life, the long and tedious race,
Hath travell'd out in lefle then 2 moncth's fpace;
Oh

Oh happie foule to whom fuch grace was given,
To make fo fhort a voyage backe to heaven,
As here a name & chriftendome t'obtaine
And to his maker then returne againe.

64. *Another.*

As carefull nurfes on their beds doe lay, (play
Their babes which would too long the wantons
So to prevent my youth's enfuing crimes
Nature my nurfe laid me to bed betimes.

65. *On a Mufitian.*

Be not offended at our fad complaint,
You quire of Angels, that have gain'd a Saint :
Where all perfection met in skill and voice,
We mourne our loffe, but yet commend your
(choyce.

66. *On Prince Henry*

Did he dye young : oh no, it could not be,
For I know few, that liv'd fo long as he.

B b 4   'Till

Till God and all men lov'd him, then be bold
The man that lives so long must needs be old.

67. *On a Cobler.*

Come hither, reade, my gentle friend !
And here behold a cobler's end.
Longer in length his life had gone,
But that he had no laste so long ;
O mighty death! whose dart can kill,
The man that made him soules at will.

68. *On Master Doe.*

Do is my name, and here I lye,
My Grammar tells me, *Do fit Di.*

69. *On a Gard'ner.*

Could hee forget his death that ev'ry houre
Was emblem'd to it, by the fading flowre ?
Should hee not mind his end ? yes sure he must
That itill was conversant 'mong beds of dust.

70. On

✦✦✦✦✦✦✦✦✦✦✦✦✦✦✦✦✦✦✦✦✦✦✦✦✦✦✦

70. *On Edmund Spencer, poet laureat.*

He was, and is (see then where lyes the odds)
Once god of Poets, Poet now to th' gods,
And though his time of life, be gone about,
The life of his lines never shall weare out.

71. *Ou Taylour a Sergeant, kill'd by a Horse.*

A Taylour is a thiefe, a Sergeant is worfe
Who here lyes dead, god-a-mercy horfe.

71. *On Sir Francis Drake, drowned.*

                   (fame
Where Drake first found, there last he loft his
And for his tombe left nothing but his name.
His body's buried under fome great wave,
The fea that was his glory, is his grave.
Of him no man, true Epitaph can make,
For who can fay, here lies Sir Francis Drake ?

73. *On*

73. *On a Drunkard.*

Byhax the drunkard, while he liv'd would say,
The more I drinke the more me think's I may:
But fee how death hath prov'd his faying juft,
For he hath drunke himfelfe as dry as duft.

74. *On a Child.*

Tread foftly paffenger ! for here doth lye
A dainty Jewell of fweet infancie :
A harmeleffe babe, that onely came & cry'd
In baptifme to bee wafht from fin and dy'd.

75. *Another.*

In this marble-casket lyes
A matchleffe jewell of rich prize
Whom nature in the worlds disda
But fhew'd and put it up againe.

76. *On Mafter Stone.*

Here worthy of a better cheft,
A pretious ftone inclos'd doth reft   Whom

Whom nature had so rarely wrought
That Pallas it admir'd and thought,
No greater jewell, than to weare
Still such a diamond in her eare :
But sicknesse did it from her wring,
And placed it in Libitina's ring,
Who changed natures worke a new
And death's pale image, in it drew.
Pitty that paine had not been sav'd,
So good a stone to be engrav'd.

77. *On Master Aire.*

Under this stone of marble fayre
Lyes th'body 'ntomb'd of Gervase Aire.
He dy'd not of an ague fitt
Nor surfetted of too much witt,
Me thinks this was a wond'rous death,
That Aire should dye for want of breath.

78. *On a young man.*

Supriz'd by griefe and sicknesse here I lye,
Stopt in my middle age and soone made dead,

                                        Yet

✤✤✤✤✤✤✤✤✤✤✤✤✤✤✤✤✤✤✤✤✤✤✤✤✤✤✤

Yet doe not grudge at God, if foone thou dye,
But know hee trebles favours on thy head.
    Who for thy morning worke, equal's thy pay,
    With thofe that have endur'd the heate of day

79. *On Mafter Sand's.*

Who would live in others breath ?
Fame deceives the dead mans truft,
When our names doe change by death ;
Sands I was and now am duft.

80. *On a Scholler.*

Some doe for anguifh weepe, for anger I,
That ignorance fhould live, and arte fhould dye.

81. *On Mafter Goad.*

Go adde this verfe, to Goad's herfe,
For Goad is gone, but whither ?
Goad himfelfe, is gone to God
'Twas death's goad drove him thither.

82. *On Master Munday.*

Hallowed be the Sabboath,
And farewell all worldly pelfe ;
The weeke begins on Tuesday,
For Munday hath hang'd himselfe.

83. *On the two Littletons who were drowned at Oxford.* 1636.

Here lye wee (reader canst thou not admire ?)
Who both at once by water dy'd and fire,
For whilst our bodies perisht in the deepe,
Our soules in love burnt, so we fell asleepe :
Let this be then our Epitaph, here lyes
Two, yet but one, one for the other dyes.

84. *On a Matron.*

Here lyes a wife was chaste, a mother blest,
A modest Matron, all these in one chest :
Sarah unto her mate, *Mary* to God,
Martha to men, whilst here she had abode.

85. *In*

85. *In Latine thus.*

Vxor caſta, parens fœlix, matrona pudica,
Sara viro, mundo Martha, Maria Deo.

86. *On a Butler.*

That death ſhould thus from hence our Butler
Into my minde it cannot quickly finke,   (catch
Sure death came thirſty to the butt'ry-hatch
When he (that buiſy'd was)deny'd him drinke.
  Tut 'twas not fo,'tis like he gave him liquor
And death made drunke, him made away the
Yet let not others grieve to much in mind(quicker
(The Butlers gone) the key's are left behind.

87. *On a Souldier.*

When I was young in warres I ſhed my blood,
Both for my King and for my countries good;
In elder yeares, my care was chiefe to be
Souldier to him that ſhed his blood for me.

88. *On*

88. *On a Tobacconist.*

Loe here I lye, roll'd up like th'Indian weede
My pipes I have pack't up, for breath I neede.
Man's breath's a vopour, he himselfe is grasse
My breath, but of a weede, the vapour was.
When I shal turne to earth, good friends! beware
Least it evap'rate and infect the ayre.

94. *On Master Thomas Allen.*

No Epitaphs neede make the just man fam'd,
The good are prays'd, when they are only nam'd

89. *On Master Cooke.*

To God, his country, and the poore, he had
A zealous Soule, free heart, and lib'rall minde.
His wife, his children, and his kindred sad
Lacke of his love, his care, and kindnesse finde :
Yet are their sorrowes asswag'd wth the thought
He hath attayn'd the happinesse he sought.

90. *On*

✤✤✤✤✤✤✤✤✤✤✤✤✤✤✤✤✤✤✤✤✤✤✤✤✤✤

90. *On a Printer whose wife was lame.*

Sleep William! sleep, she that thine eyes did close
Makes lame *Iambiques* for thee, as shee goes.

91. *On a Taylour who dy'd of the stitch.*

Here lyes a Taylour in this ditch,
Who liv'd and dyed by the stitch.

92. *On a dumbe fellow dying of the collick.*

Here lyes *Iohn Dumbello,*
Who dy'd becaufe he was fo
For if his breech could have fpoke,
His heart furely had not broke.

92. *On Ifabella a Curtezan.*

He who would write an Epitaph
Whereby to make faire Is'bell laugh,
Muft get upon her, and write well
Here underneath lyes Ifabell.

✠✠✠✠✠✠✠✠✠✠✠✠✠✠✠✠✠✠✠✠✠✠

94. *On a vertuous wife, viz. Susanna wife to Mr. William Horsenell.*

In briefe, to speake thy praise let this suffice,
Thou wert a wife, most loving, modest, wise;
Of children carefull, to thy neighbour's
A worthy mistris and of liberall mind.   (kind,

95. *On Mr. Christopher Lawson.*

Death did not kill unjustly this good-man,
But death in death by death did shew his power,
His pious deedes & thoughts to heaven fore-ran;
There to prepare his soule a blessed bower.

96. *On Hobson the Carrier.*

Here Hobson lyes amongst his many betters,
A man unlearned, yet a man of letters,
His carriage was well knowne, oft hath he gone
In Embassye 'twixt father and the sonne;   (ken
There's few in Cambridge, to his praise be it spo-
But may remember him, by some good token:
From whence he rid to London day by day,
Till death benighting him, he lost his way,

C c   His

✦✦✦✦✦✦✦✦✦✦✦✦✦✦✦✦✦✦✦✦✦✦✦✦✦✦✦✦

His teame was of the best, nor would he have
Bence mir'd in any way, but in the grave.
Nor is't a wonder, that he thus is gone,
Since all men knew, he long was drawing on.
Thus rest in peace thou everlasting swaine
And supreame waggoner, next Charles his
(wayne.

97. *On a Welshman.*

Here lyes puried under these stones
Shon ap Williams ap Ienkyn ap Iones,
Her was porne in Wales, her was kill'd in Franc.
Her went to Cott py a fery mischance,
Layce now.

98. *On M. Pricke.*

Vpon the fith day of November
Christ's Colledge lost a privie member
Cupid and death did both their arrowes micke,
Cupid shot shore, but death did hit the pricke.
Women lament and maidons make great mones
Because the Pricke is laid beneath the stones.

99. *On a Porter.*

At length by worke of wond'rous fate
Here lyes the potter of Wynchester-gate

If

If gone to heav'n, as much I feare,
He can be but a porter there :
He fear'd not hell so much for's sinne,
As for th' great rapping and oft comming in.

100. *On M. Carter, burnt by the great powder-*
mischance in Finsbury.

Here lyes an honest Carter (yet no clowne)
Vnladen of his cares, his end the crowne,
Vanisht from hence even in a cloud of smoake,
A blowne-up Citizen, and yet not broke.

101. *On a Lady dying in Child-bed.*

Borne at the first to bring another forth, (worth
Shee leaves the world, to leave the world her
Thus Phænix-like, as sue was borne to bleede
Dying herselfe, renew's it in her seede.

102. *On Prince Henry.*

Loe where he shineth yonder
A fixed starre in heaven,
Whose motions thence, coms under
None of the Planets seven :

If

❀ ❀❀❀❀ ❀❀❀❀❀❀❀❀❀❀❀❀❀❀❀❀❀❀❀❀❀❀

I' that the Moone fhou'd tender,
   The Sunne her love and marry,
They both could not engender,
   So bright a ftarre as Harry.

10. *Vpon one, who dy'd in prifon.*

Reader, I liv'd, enquire no more,
Leaſt a fpye enter in at doore,
Such are the times a dead-man dare
Not truſt or creditt common ayre :
But dye, and lye entombed here,
By me, I'le whifper in thine eare
Such things as onely duſt to duſt,
(And without witneffe) may entruſt.

14. *On Sir Walter Rawleygh.*

If fpite be pleas'd, when as her objeﬅ's dead,
Or Malice pleas'd, when it hath bruiz'd the head
Or envie pleas'd, when it hath what it would,
Then all are pleas'd, for Rawleyh's blood is cold,
Which were it warme & aﬅive would o'recome
And ſtrike the two fuſt blind, the other dumbe.

(Quoth he) this is as good as one of steele,
For me to knock now into fortunes wheele.

501 *Three Pages.*

Three Pages on a time together met,
And made a motion, that each one would let
The other know what hee'd desire to be
Having his wish, thereto they did agree.
Quoth one, to be a Melon I would chuse,
For then I'm sure, none would refuse
To kisse my breech although the sent were hot,
And so they'd know whether I were good or not.

502 *A Gentleman and his Phisitian.*

A Gentleman not richest in discretion,
Was alwayes sending for his own phisition.
And on a time he needs would of him know,
What was the cause his pulse did go so slow?
Why (quoth the Doctor) thus it comes to passe,
Must needs go slow, which goes upon an asse.

M 2   503

❧❀❧❀❧❀❧❀❧❀❧❀❧❀❧❀❧❀❧❀❧❀❧❀❧❀❧

503 *A Peasant and his wife.*

A Peasant with his wife was almost wilde,
To understand his Daughter was with childe,
And said if to the girle sh'ad taken heed,
Sh'ad not been guilty of so foule a deed.
Husband (said she) I sweare by cock,
   (Welfare a good old token)
The Dev'll him selfe can't keep that lock
   Which every key can open.

504 *G-L-Asse.*

He that loves Glasse without a G,
Leave out L and that is hee.

—Nihil hic nisi carmina desunt.

EPITAPHS.

1. *On a travelling begger.*

HEre lies a Vagrant person whom our lawes,
(Of late growne strict)denied passage, cause
Hee wandred thus, therefore returne he must,
From whence at first he hither came, to dust.

2. *On a Mason.*

So long the Mason wrought on other's walles,
That his owne house of clay to ruine falles :
No wonder spitefull death, wrought his annoy,
He us'd to build, and death seekes to destroy.

A a   3. On

3. *On a Dyer.*

Though death the Dyer colour-leſſe hath made,
Yet he dies pale ; and will not leave his trade ;
But being dead, the meanes yet doth not lacke
To die his friends cloth into mourning blacke.
Some ſure foreſaw his death, for they of late
Vs'd to exclaime upon his dying fate.   (been,
And weake, and faint,he ſeem'd oft-times t'have
For to change colours, often he was ſeen ;
Yet there no matter was ſo foule, but he
Would ſet a colour on it handſomlye.
Death him no unexpected ſtroke could give
That learnt to dye, ſince he began to live.
He ſhall yet prove, what he before hath try'd,
And ſhall once more, live after he hath dy'd.

4. *Of a Schoolemaſter.*

The grämer Schoole a long time taught I have,
Yet all my skill could not decline the grave,
But yet I hope it one day will be ſhow'ne
In no caſe ſave the Ablative alone.

✠✠✠✠✠✠✠✠✠✠✠✠✠✠✠✠✠✠✠✠✠✠✠✠✠✠✠

5. *On William Shake-jpeare.*

Renowned Spencer lye a thought more nigh,
To learned Chaucer, and rare Beaumont lye
A little neerer Spencer, to make roome   (tombe
For Shake-fpeare in your threefold, fourefold
To lodge all foure in one bed make a fhift
Vntill Doomes day, for hardly will a fifth
Betwixt this day and that by Fates be flaine,
For whom your curtaines may be drawn againe.
If your precedencie in death doe barre
A fourth place in your facred Sepulchre;
Vnder this facred marble of thine owne,
Sleepe rare Tragædian Shake-fpeare! fleep alone.
Thy unmolefted peace in an unfhared cave
Poffeffe as Lord, not tenant of thy grave,
That unto us, and others it may bee
Honour hereafter to be laid by thee.

6. *On a youth.*

Now thou haft Heaven for merit, but 'tis ftrange
Mortality fhould envie at thy change :
But God thought us unfit, for fuch as thee,
And made thee confort of eternitye.

❖❖❖❖❖❖❖❖❖❖❖❖❖❖❖❖❖❖❖❖❖❖❖❖❖❖❖

We grieve not then,that thou to heaven art tak
But that thou haft thy friends fo foone forfaken

7. *On Prince Henry.*

I have no veine in verfe, but if I cou'd,
Diftill on every word a pearle I would.   (ers,
Our forrowes pearles drop not from pens ; but
Whilft other's Mufe ? write, mine onely cries.

8. *On a Foot-boy that dyed with*
overmuch running.

Bafe tyrant death thus to affaile one tyr'd
Who fcarfe his lateft breath beeing left expir'd ;
And being too too cruell thus to ftay
So fwift a courfe,at length ran quite away.
But pretty boy, be fure it was not death
That left behind thy body out of breath :
Thy foule and body running in a race,
Thy foule held out ; thy body tyr'd apace,
Thy foule gained, and left that lump of clay
To reft it felfe, untill the latter day

The rash fate cri'd here, as appeares,
  Counting his vertues for his yeares,
  His goodnesse made them so o're seene,
    Vhich shew'd him threescore;at eighteene.

Enquire not his disease or paine!
  He dy'd of nothing else but spayne,
Where the worst calenture he feeles,
  Are Jesuites,and Alguaziles,
  Where he is not allow'd to have,
    (Vnlesse he steal't) a quiet grave.

Hee needes no other Epitaph or stone
  But this, here lyes lov'd Washington,
Write this in teares, in that loose dust
  And every greiv'd beholder must,
  When he waighs him,and knowes his yeares.
    Renew the letters with his teares.

126. On *Gustavus Adolphus*, *King of Sweden.*

The world expects Swede's monumentall stone,
Should equall the Philosophers, each groane
                    Should

❖❖❖❖❖❖❖❖❖❖❖❖❖❖❖❖❖❖❖❖❖❖❖❖❖❖❖

Should breath a golden veine, and ev'ry verse
Should draw Elixar from his fatall hearfe.
No fitter fubject where ftrong lines fhould meet
Than fuch a noble center; could the feet
Of able verfe but trace his rectories,
They neede not feare o're ftrayn'd Hyperbole's,
Where all's tranfcendent, who out-paralell'd
Plutarch's felected Heroes; and is held
The tenth of Worthies, who hath over-acted
Great *Cæfar's* German comments, & contracted
His expeditions by preventing awe,
He often over-came before hee faw;
And (what of his great fonne Jove us'd to fay)
Hee alwaies either found or made his way.
Such was his perfonall and fingle fight,
As if that death it felfe had ta'ne her flight
Into brave Swedens fcabbard, when he drew;
Death with that fteele inevitably flew;
His campe a church, wherein the Gen'rall's life
Was the beft Sermon; and the onely ftrife
'Amongft his was to repeate it, bended knee
Was his prime pofture, and his enemy
Found this moft prævalent, his difcipline
Impartiall and exact, it did out-fhine
Thofe antique Martiall-Græcian, Roman lamps
From wch moft of the worlds fucceeding camps
Have

Have had their borrow'd light; this, this was hee
All this and more, yet even all this can dye.
Death surely ventur'd on the Swede' to try
If heav'n were subject to mortality;
And shot his soule to heav'n, as if that shee
Could(if not kill)unthrone a diety
Bold death's deceiv'd, 'tis in another sense
That heav'n is said to suffer violence.
No yr'n chaine-shot, but 'tis the golden chaine
Of vertue and the Graces, are the maine
That doe unhinge the everlasting gates
All which like yoaked undivided mates, (chain'd
Were linck't in Sweden, where they were en-
Like Orthodoxall volumes nothing feign'd,
Though fairely bound his story is not dipt
In oyle, but in his owne true Manuscript.
It is enough to name him, surely wee
Have got that Roman's doating Lethargy
And may our names forget, if so we can
Forget the name of Sweden; renown'd man !
Thou hadst no sooner made the Worthies ten
But heavē did claime the tenth; zealous that men
Would idolize thee, but their instument.
Thus thy Meridian prov'd thy Occiden.
Had longer dayes beene graunted by the fates,
Rome had heard this *Hanniball* at her gates
                                                  Fare-

Farewell thou Auftrian fcourge,
    thou moderne wonder,
Srange raine hath followed
    thy laft clap of thunder,
A fhower of teares :
    and yet for ought we know ,
The Horne that's left.
    may blow downe Jericho

F I N I S.

Octob. 8. 1639.   *Jmprimatur.*

Matth. Clar.

OVTLANDISH
PROVERBS,
SELECTED

LONDON,

Printed by *T. P.* for *Humphrey Blunden*; at the *Castle in Corn-hill.* 1640.

Outlandiſh
PROVERBS.

1. **M**AN Propoſeth, God diſ-
poſeth.

      2. Hee begins to die,
that quits his deſires.

      3. A handfull of good
life, is better then a buſhell of learning.

    4. He that ſtudies his content, wants
it.

    5. Every day brings his bread with it.

    6. Humble Hearts, have humble de-
ſires.

    7. Hee that ſtumbles and falles not,
mends his pace.

    8 The Houſe ſhewes the owner.

    9. Hee that gets out of debt, growes
rich.

    10. All is well with him, who is belo-

ved

❖❖❖❖❖❖❖❖❖❖❖❖❖❖❖❖❖❖❖❖❖

ved of his neighbours.

11. Building and marrying of Children, are great wasters.

12. A good bargaine is a pick-purse.

13. The scalded dog feares cold water.

14. Pleasing ware, is halfe sould.

15 Light burthens, long borne,growe heavie.

16. The Wolfe knowes, what the ill beast thinkes.

17 Who hath none to still him, may weepe out his eyes.

18. When all sinnes growes old,cove-teousnesse is young.

19. If yee would know a knave,give him a staffe.

20. You cannot know wine by the bar-rell.

21. A coole mouth, and warme feet, live long.

22 A Horse made,and a man to make.

23 Looke not for muske in a dogges kennell.

24. Not a long day, but a good heart rids worke.

25. Hee puls with a long rope, that waights for anothers death.

26.Great

26. Great ſtrokes make not ſweete muſick.

27. A caske and an ill cuſtome muſt be broken.

28. A fat houſe-keeper, makes leane Executors.

29 Empty Chambers, make fooliſh maides.

30. The gentle Hawke, halfe mans her ſelfe.

31. The Devill is not alwaies at one doore.

32. When a friend askes, there is no, to morrow.

33. God ſends cold, according to Cloathes.

34 One ſound blow will ſerve to undo us all.

35. Hee looſeth nothing, that looſeth not God.

36. The Germans wit, is in his fingers.

37 At dinner my man appeares.

38. Who gives to all, denies all.

39. Quick beleevers neede broad ſhoulders.

40 Who remove ſtones, bruiſe their fingers.

41. All

❖❖❖❖❖❖❖❖❖❖❖❖❖❖❖❖❖❖❖❖❖❖❖❖❖

41. All came from, and will goe to o-
thers.

42. He that will take the bird, muſt not
skare it.

43. He lives unſafely, that lookes too
neere on things.

44. A gentle houſwife, marres the houſ-
hold.

45. A crooked log makes a ſtrait fire.

46. He hath great neede of a fooꝛ, that
plaies the foole himſelfe.

47. A Marchant that gaines not, loo-
feth.

48. Let not him that feares feathers,
come among wild-foule.

49. Love, and a Cough cannot be hid.

50. A Dwarie, on a Gyants ſhoulder,
fees further of the two.

51. Hee that ſends a foole, means to
follow him.

52. Brabling Curres never want fore
eares.

53. Better the feet ſlip then the tongue.

54. For waſhing his hands, none ſels
his lands.

55. A Lyons skin is never cheape.

56. The goate muſt browſe where ſhe
is tyed.   57. Who

✤✦✤✦✤✦✤✦✤✦✤✦✤✦✤✦✤✦✤✦✤

57 Who hath a Wolfe for his mate, needes a Dog for his man

58. In a good house all is quickly ready.

59. A bad dog never sees the Wolfe.

60. God oft hath a great share in a little house.

61. Ill ware is never cheape.

62. A cherefull looke, makes a dish a feast.

63. If all fooles had bables, wee should want fuell.

64. Vertue never growes old.

65. Evening words are not like to morning.

66. Were there no fooles, badd ware would not passe.

67. Never had ill workeman good tooles.

68. Hee stands not surely, that never slips.

69. Were there no hearers, there would be no backbiters.

70. Every thing is of use to a houskeeper.

71. When prayers are done, my Lady is ready.

A 4   72. A

✤✤✤ ✤✤✤✤✤✤✤✤✤✤✤✤✤✤ ✤✤✤ ✤✤✤✤

72. At Length the Fox turnes Monk.

73. Flies are busiest about leane horses.

74. Harken to reason or shee will bee heard.

75 The bird loves her nest.

76 Every thing new, is fine.

77. When a dog is a drowning, every one offers him drink.

78. Better a bare foote then none.

79 Who is so deafe, as he that will not heare.

80 He that is warme, thinkes all so.

81. At length the Fox is brought to the Furrier.

82. Hee that goes barefoot, must not plant thornes.

83. They that are booted are not alwaes ready.

84. He that will learne to pray, let him goe to Sea.

85. In spending, lies the advantage.

86. Hee that lives well is learned enough.

87. Ill vessells seldome miscarry.

88. A full belly neither fights nor flies well.

89. All truths are not to be told.

90. An

✿✿✿✿✿✿✿ ✿✿✿✿✿ ✿✿✿✿✿✿✿✿✿✿✿

90 An old wise mans shaddow, is better then a young buzzards sword.

91. Noble houskeepers neede no dores.

92. Every ill man hath his ill day.

93. Sleepe without supping, and wake without owing

94. I gave the mouse a hole, and she is become my heire.

95. Assaile who will, the valiant attends.

96. Whether goest griefe ? where I am wont.

97. Praise day at night, and life at the end.

98. Whether shall the Oxe goe, where he shall not labour

99. Where you thinke there is bacon, there is no Chimney.

100 Mend your cloathes, and you may hold out this yeare.

101. Presse a stick, and it seemes a youth.

02. The tongue walkes where the teeth speede not.

103. A faire wife and a frontire Castle breede quarrels,

104. Leave jesting whiles it pleaseth, lest it turne to earnest.   105.De-

✢✢✢✢✢✢✢✢✢✢✢✢✢✢✢✢✢✢✢✢✢

105. Deceive not thy Phyſitian, Con-feſſor, nor Lawyer.

106. Ill natures, the more you aske them, the more they ſtick.

107. Vertue and a Trade are the beſt portion for Children.

108. The Chicken is the Countries, but the Citie eateth it.

109. He that gives thee a Capon, give him the leg and the wing.

110. Hee that lives ill, feare followes him.

111. Give a clowne your finger, and he will take your hand.

112. Good is to bee ſought out, and e-vill attended.

113. A good pay-maſter ſtarts not at aſſurances.

114. No Alchymy to ſaving.

115. To a grate full man give mony when he askes.

116. Who would doe ill ne're wants occaſion.

117. To fine folkes a little ill finely wrapt.

118. A child correct behind and not before.

119. To

119. To a faire day open the window, but make you ready as to a foule.

120. Keepe good men company, and you shall be of the number.

121. No love to a Fathers.

122. The Mill gets by going.

123. To a boyling pot flies come not.

124. Make hast to an ill way that you may get out of it.

125. A snow yeare, a rich yeare.

126. Better to be blinde, then to see ill.

127. Learne weeping, and thou shalt laugh gayning.

128. Who hath no more bread then neede, must not keepe a dog.

129. A garden must be lookt unto and drest as the body.

130. The Fox, when hee cannot reach the grapes, saies they are not ripe.

131. Water trotted is as good as oates.

132. Though the Mastiffe be gentle, yet bite him not by the lippe.

133. Though a lie be well drest, it is ever overcome.

134. Though old and wise, yet still advise.

135. Three helping one another, beare the burthen of sixe.   136. Old

❖❖❖❖❖❖❖❖❖❖❖❖❖❖❖❖❖❖❖❖❖❖❖❖

136. Old wine, and an old friend, are good provisions.

137. Happie is hee that chastens himselfe.

138. Well may hee smell fire, whose gowne burnes.

139. The wrongs of a Husband or Master are not reproached.

140 Welcome evill, if thou commest alone.

141. Love your neighbour, yet pull not downe your hedge.

142. The bit that one eates, no friend makes.

143. A drunkards purse is a bottle.

144. Shee spins well that breedes her children.

145. Good is the *mora* that makes all sure.

146. Play with a foole at home, and he will play with you in the market.

147. Every one stretcheth his legges according to his coverlet.

148. Autumnall Agues are long, or mortall.

149 Marry your sonne when you will; your daughter when you can.

150. Dally

✣✤✣✤✣✤✣✤✣✤✣✤✣✤✣✤✣✤✣✤

150. Dally not with mony or women.

151. Men speake of the faire, as things went with them there.

152. The best remedy against an ill man, is much ground betweene both.

143. The mill cannot grind with the water that's past.

154. Corne is cleaned with winde, and the foule with chastnings.

155 Good words are worth much, and cost little.

156. To buy deare is not bounty.

157. Jest not with the eye or with Religion.

158. The eye and Religion can beare no jesting.

159. Without favour none will know you, and with it you will not know your selfe.

160. Buy at a faire, but sell at home.

161. Cover your selfe with your shield, and care not for cryes.

162. A wicked mans gift hath a touch of his master.

163. None is a foole alwaies, every one sometimes.

164. From a chollerick man withdraw

a

✤✤✤✤✤✤✤✤✤✤✤✤✤✤✤✤✤✤✤✤✤✤✤✤✤

a little, from him that faies nothing, for ever.

165. Debters are lyers.

166. Of all fmells, bread : of all tafts, falt.

167. In a great River great fifh are found, but take heede, left you bee drowned.

168. Ever fince we weare cloathes, we know not one another.

169. God heales, and the Phyfitian hath the thankes.

170. Hell is full of good meanings and wifhings.

171. Take heede of ftill waters, the quick paffe away.

172. After the houfe is finifht, leave it.

173. Our owne actions are our fecurity, not others judgements.

178. Thinke of eafe, but worke on.

179. Hee that lies long a bed his eftate feeles it.

180. Whether you boyle fnow or pound it, you can have but water of it.

181. One ftroke fells not an oke.

182. God complaines not, but doth what is fitting.

183. A

❖❖❖❖❖❖❖❖❖❖❖❖❖❖❖❖❖❖❖❖❖❖❖❖

183. A diligent Shcoller and the Ma-
ster's paid.

184. Milke saies to wine, welcome
friend.

185. They that know one another, sa-
lute a farre off.

186. Where there is no honour, there
is no griefe.

187. Where the drink goes in, there the
wit goes out.

188. He that staies does the businesse.

189 Almes never make poore others.

190. Great almes-giving lessens no
mans living.

191. Giving much to the poore, doth
inrich a mans store.

192. It takes much from the account,
to which his sir doth amount.

193. It adds to the glory both of soule
and body.

194 Ill comes in by ells, and goes
out by inches.

195. The Smith and his penny both are
black.

196 Whose house is of glasse, must
not throw stones at another.

197. If the old dog barke he gives coun-
sell.   198. The

❖❖❖❖❖❖❖❖❖❖❖❖❖❖❖❖❖❖❖❖❖❖

198. The tree that growes ſlowly, keepes it ſelfe for another.

199. I wept when I was borne, and every day ſhewes why.

200. Hee that lookes not before, finds himſelfe behind.

201. He that plaies his mony ought not to value it.

202. He that riſeth firſt, is firſt dreſt.

203. Diſeaſes of the eye are to bee cured with the elbow.

204. The hole calls the thiefe.

205. A gentlemans grayhound, and a ſalt-box; ſeeke them at the fire.

206. A childs ſervice is little, yet hee is no little foole that deſpiſeth it.

207. The river paſt, and God forgotten.

208. Evils have their comfort; good none can ſupport(to wit)with a moderate and contented heart.

209. Who muſt account for himſelfe and others, muſt know both.

210. Hee that eats the hard ſhall eate the ripe.

211. The miſerable man makes a peny of a farthing, and the liberall of a farthing ſixe pence.   212. The

✦✦✦✦✦✦✦✦✦✦✦✦✦✦✦✦✦✦✦✦✦✦

212. The honey is ſweet, but the Bee ſtings.

213. Waight and meaſure take away ſtrife.

214. The ſonne full and tattered, the daughter empty and fine.

215. Every path hath a puddle.

216. In good yeares corne is hay, in ill yeares ſtraw is corne.

217. Send a wiſe man on an errand, and ſay nothing unto him.

218. In life you lov'd me not, in death you bewaile me.

219. Into a mouth ſhut, flies flie not.

220. The hearts letter is read in the eyes

221. The ill that comes out of our mouth falles into our boſome.

222. In great pedigrees there are Governours and Chandlers.

223. In the houſe of a Fidler, all fiddle.

224. Sometimes the beſt gaine is to loſe.

225. Working and making a fire doth diſcretion require.

226. One graine fills not a ſacke, but helpes his fellowes.

B   227. I ſ

✤✤✤✤✤✤✤✤✤✤✤✤✤✤✤✤✤✤✤✤✤✤✤

227. It is a great victory that comes without blood.

228. In war, hunting, and love, men for one pleaſure a thouſand griefes prove.

229. Reckon right, and February hath one and thirty daies.

230. Honour without profit is a ring on the finger.

231. Eſtate in two pariſhes is bread in two wallets.

232. Honour and profit lie not in one ſacke.

233. A naughty child is better ſick, then whole.

234. Truth and oyle are ever above.

235. He that riſeth betimes hath ſome thing in his head.

236. Adviſe none to marry or to goe to warre.

237. To ſteale the Hog, and give the feet for almes.

238. The thorne comes forth with his point forwards.

239. One hand waſheth another, and both the face.

240. The fault of the horſe is put on the ſaddle.

241. The

✚✚✚✚✚✚✚✚✚✚✚✚✚✚✚✚✚✚✚✚

241. The corne hides it felf in the fnow, as an old man in furrs.

242. The Jewes fpend at Eafter, the Mores at marriages, the Chriftians in futes.

243. Fine dreffing is a foule houfe fwept before the doores.

244. A woman and a glaffe are ever in danger.

245. An ill wound is cured, not an ill name.

246. The wife hand doth not all that the foolifh mouth fpeakes.

247. On painting and fighting looke a-loofe.

248. Knowledge is folly, except grace guide it.

249. Punifhment is lame, but it comes.

250. The more women looke in their glaffe, the leffe they looke to their houfe.

251. A long tongue is a figne of a fhort hand.

252. Marry a widdow before fhe leave mourning.

253. The worft of law is, that one fuit breedes twenty.

B 2   254. Pro-

✤✤✤✤✤✤✤✤✤✤✤✤✤✤✤✤✤✤✤✤✤

254. Providence is better then a rent.

255. What your glaſſe telles you, will not be told by Councell.

256. There are more men threatned then ſtricken.

257. A foole knowes more in his houſe, then a wiſe man in anothers.

258. I had rather ride on an aſſe that carries me, then a horſe that throwes me.

259. The hard gives more then he that hath nothing.

260. The beaſt that goes alwaies never wants blowes.

261. Good cheape is deare.

262. It coſts more to doe ill then to doe well.

263. Good words quench more then a a bucket of water.

264. An ill agreement is better then a good judgement.

265. There is more talke then trouble.

266. Better ſpare to have of thine own, then aske of other men.

267. Better good afarre off, then evill at hand.

268. Feare keepes the garden better, then the gardiner.

269. I

✤✤✤✤✤✤✤✤✤✤✤✤✤✤✤✤✤✤✤✤✤✤

269. I had rather aske of my sire browne bread, then borrow of my neighbour white.

270. Your pot broken seemes better then my whole one.

271. Let an ill man lie in thy straw, and he lookes to be thy heire.

272. By suppers more have beene killed then *Gallen* ever cured.

273. While the discreet advise the foole doth his busines.

274. A mountaine and a river are good neighbours.

275. Gossips are frogs, they drinke and talke.

276. Much spends the traveller, more then the abider.

277. Prayers and provender hinder no journey.

278. A well-bred youth neither speakes of himselfe, nor being spoken to is silent.

279. A journying woman speakes much of all, and all of her.

280. The Fox knowes much, but more he that catcheth him.

281. Many friends in generall, one in speciall.

B 3   282. The

✤✤✤✤✤✤✤✤✤✤✤✤✤✤✤✤✤✤✤✤✤✤✤

282. The foole askes much, but hee is more foole that grants it.

283. Many kiſſe the hand,they wiſh cut off.

284. Neither bribe nor looſe thy right.

285. In the world who knowes not to ſwimme,goes to the bottome.

286. Chuſe not an houſe neere an Inne, (viz for noiſe) or in a corner (for filth.)

287. Hee is a foole that thinks not, that another thinks.

288. Neither eyes on letters, nor hands in coffers.

289. The Lyon is not ſo fierce as they paint him.

290. Goe not for every griefe to the Phyſitian, nor for every quarrell to the Lawyer, nor for every thirſt to the pot.

291. Good ſervice is a great inchant-ment.

292. There would bee no great ones if there were no little ones.

293. It's no ſure rule to fiſh with a croſ-bow.

294. There were no ill language, if it were not ill taken.

295. The groundſell ſpeakes not ſave what

what it heard at the hinges.

296. The best mirrour is an old friend.

297. Say no ill of the yeere, till it be past.

298. A mans discontent is his worst e-
vill.

299 Feare nothing but sinne.

300. The child saies nothing, but what it
heard by the fire.

301. Call me not an olive, till thou see me
gathered.

302. That is not good language which
all understand not.

303. Hee that burnes his house warmes
himselfe for once.

304. He will burne his house, to warme
his hands.

305. Hee will spend a whole yeares rent
at one meales meate.

306. All is not gold that glisters.

307. A blustering night, a faire day.

308. Bee not idle and you shall not bee
longing.

309. He is not poore that hath little, but
he that desireth much.

310. Let none say, I will not drinke wa-
ter,

311. Hee wrongs not an old man that
B 4   steales

✧✧✧✧✧✧✧✧✧✧✧✧✧ ✧✧✧✧✧✧✧✧✧✧

ſtcales his ſupper from him.

312. The tongue talkes at the heads coſt.

313. Hee that ſtrikes with his tongue, muſt ward with his head.

314. Keep not ill men company, leſt you increaſe the number.

315. God ſtrikes not with both hands, for to the ſea he made havens , and to rivers foords.

316. A rugged ſtone growes ſmooth from hand to hand.

317. No lock will hold againſt the power of gold.

318. The abſent partie is ſtill fault ie.

319. Peace , and Patience, and death with repentance.

320. If vou loofe your time, you cannot get mony nor gaine.

321. Bee not a Baker, if your head be of butter

322. Aske much to have a little.

323. Litle ſtickes kindle the fire ; great on. put it out.

324. Anothers bread coſts deare.

325. Although it raine, throw not away thy watering pot.

326. Although

✤✤✤✤✤✤✤✤✤✤✤✤✤✤✤✤✤✤✤✤✤

326. Although the sun shine, leave not thy cloake at home.

327. A little with quiet is the onely dyet.

328. In vaine is the mill clacke, if the Miller his hearing lack.

329. By the needle you shall draw the thread, and by that which is past, see how that which is to come will be drawne on.

330. Stay a little and news will find you.

331. Stay till the lame messenger come, if you will know the truth of the thing.

332. When God will, no winde, but brings raine.

333. Though you rise early, yet the day comes at his time, and not till then.

334. Pull downe your hatt on the winds side.

335. As the yeere is, your pot must seeth.

336. Since you know all, and I nothing, tell me what I dreamed last n.ght.

337. When the Foxe preacheth, beware geese.

338. When you are an Anvill, hold you still; when you are a hammer strike your fill.

339. Poore and liberall, rich and coveteous.

340. He

✤✤✤✤✤✤✤✤✤✤✤✤✤✤✤✤✤✤✤✤✤✤✤

340. He that makes his bed ill, lies there.

341. Hee that labours and thrives spins gold.

342. He that sowes trusts in God.

343. Hee that lies with the dogs, riseth with fleas.

344. Hee that repaires not a part, builds all.

345. A discontented man kwes not where to sit easie.

346. Who spits against heaven, it falls in his face.

347. Hee that dines and leaves, layes the cloth twice.

348. Who eates his cock alone must saddle his horse alone.

349. He that is not handsome at 20, nor strong at 30, nor rich at 40, nor wise at 50 will never bee handsome, strong, rich, or wise.

350. Hee that doth what hee will, doth not what he ought.

351. Hee that will deceive the fox, must rise betimes.

352. He that lives well sees a farre off.

353. He that hath a mouth of his owne, must not say to another; Blow.

354. He

✠✦✠✦✠✦✠✦✠✦✠✦✠✦✠✦✠✦✠✦✠✦

354. He that will be served must bee patient.

355. Hee that gives thee a bone, would not have thee die.

356. He that chastens one, chastens 20.

357. He that hath lost his credit is dead to the world.

358. He that hath no ill fortune, is troubled with good.

359. Hee that demands misseth not, unlesse his demands be foolish.

360. He that hath no hony in his pot, let him have it in his mouth.

361. He that takes not up a pin, slights his wife.

362. He that owes nothing, if he makes not mouthes at us, is courteous.

363. Hee that looseth his due, gets not thankes.

364. Hee that beleeveth all, misseth, hee that beleeveth nothing, hitts not.

365. Pardons and pleasantnesse are great revenges of slanders.

366. A married man turnes his staffe into a stake.

367. If you would know secrets, looke them in griefe or pleasure.

368. Serve

✤✤✤✤✤✤✤✤✤✤✤✤✤✤✤✤✤✤✤✤✤✤✤✤

368. Serve a noble diſpoſition, though poore, the time comes that hee will repay thee.

369. The fault is as great as hee that is faulty.

370. If folly were griefe every houſe would weepe.

371. Hee that would bee well old, muſt bee old betimes.

372. Sit in your place and none can make you riſe.

373. If you could runne, as you drinke, you might catch a hare.

374. Would you know what mony is, Go borrow ſome.

375. The morning Sunne never laſts a day.

376. Thou haſt death in thy houſe, and doſt bew aile anothers.

377. All griefes with bread are leſſe.

378. All things require ſkill, but an appetite.

379. All things have their place, knew wee, how to place them.

380. Little pitchers have wide eares.

381. We are fooles one to another.

382. This world is nothing except it tend to another.   383. There

✦✦✦✦✦✦✦✦✦✦✦✦✦✦✦✦✦✦✦✦✦✦✦

383. There are three waies, the Vniver-
fities, the Sea, the Court.

384. God comes to fee without a bell.

385. Life without a friend is death with-
out a witneffe.

386. Cloath thee in war , arme thee in
peace.

387. The horfe thinkes one thing, and he
that fadles him another.

388. Mills and wives ever want.

389. The dog that licks afhes, truft not
with meale.

390. The buyer needes a hundred eyes,
the feller not one.

391. He carries well, to whom it waighes
not.

392. The comforters head never akes.

393. Step after ftep the ladder is afcen-
ded.

394. Who likes not the drinke, God de-
prives him of bread.

395. To a crazy fhip all winds are con-
trary.

396. Juftice pleafeth few in their owne
houfe.

397. In times comes he, whom God
fends.

398. Water

❖❖❖❖❖❖❖❖❖❖❖❖❖❖❖❖❖❖❖❖❖❖❖❖❖

398. Water a farre off quencheth not fire.

399. In sports and journeys men are knowne.

400. An old friend is a new house.

401. Love is not found in the market.

402. Dry feet, warme head, bring safe to bed.

403. Hee is rich enough that wants nothing.

404. One father is enough to governe one hundred sons, but not a hundred sons one father.

405. Farre shooting never kild bird.

406. An upbraided morsell never choaked any.

407. Dearths foreseene come not.

408. An ill labourer quarrells with his tooles.

409. Hee that falles into the durt, the longer he stayes there, the fowler he is.

410. He that blames would buy.

411. He that sings on friday, will weepe on Sunday.

412. The charges of building, and making of gardens are unknowne.

413. My

413. My houfe, my houfe, though thou art fmall, thou art to me the Efcuriall.

414. A hundred loade of thought will not pay one of debts.

415. Hee that comes of a hen muft fcrape.

416. He that feekes trouble never miffes.

417. He that once deceives is ever fufpected.

418. Being on fea faile, being on land fettle.

419. Who doth his owne bufineffe, foules not his hands.

420. Hee that makes a good warre makes a good peace.

421. Hee that workes after his owne manner, his head akes not at the matter.

422. Who hath bitter in his mouth, fpits not all fweet.

423. He that hath children, all his morfels are not his owne.

424. He that hath the fpice, may feafon as he lift.

425. He that hath a head of waxe muft not walke in the funne.

426. Hee

✦✦✦✦✦✦✦✦✦✦✦✦✦✦✦✦✦✦✦✦✦✦✦

426 He that hath love in his breſt, hath ſpurres in his ſides.

427. Hee that reſpects not, is not reſpected.

428. Hee that hath a Fox for his mate, hath neede of a net at his girdle.

429. He that hath right, feares, he that hath wrong, hopes.

430. Hee that hath patience hath fatt thruſhes for a farthing.

431. Never was ſtrumpet faire.

432. He that meaſures not himſelfe, is meaſured.

433. Hee that hath one hogge makes him fat, and hee that hath one ſon makes him a foole.

434. Who letts his wife goe to every feaſt, and his horſe drinke at every water, ſhall neither have good wife nor good horſe.

435. He that ſpeakes ſowes, and he that holds his peace, gathers.

436. He that hath little is the leſſe durtie.

437. He that lives moſt dies moſt.

438. He that hath one foot in the ſtraw, hath another in the ſpittle.

439. He

439. Hee that's fed at anothers hand may stay long ere he be full.

440. Hee that makes a thing too fine, breakes it.

441. Hee that bewailes himselfe hath the cure in his hands.

442. He that would be well, needs not goe from his owne house.

443. Councell breakes not the head.

444. Fly the pleasure that bites to morrow.

445. Hee that knowes what may bee gained in a day never steales.

446. Mony refused looseth its brightnesse.

447. Health and mony goe farre.

448. Where your will is ready, your feete are light.

449. A great ship askes deepe waters.

450. Woe to the house where there is no chiding.

451. Take heede of the viniger of sweet wine.

452. Fooles bite one another, but wisemen agree together.

453. Trust not one nights ice.

454. Good is good, but better carries it.

C   455. To

✠✠✠✠✠✠✠✠✠✠✠✠✠✠✠✠✠✠✠✠✠✠

455. To gaine teacheth how to ſpend.

456. Good finds good.

457. The dog gnawes the bone be-
cauſe he cannot ſwallow it.

458. The crow bewailes the ſheepe,
and then eates it.

459 Building is a ſweet impoveriſhing.

460. The firſt degree of folly is to hold
ones ſelfe wiſe, the ſecond to profeſſe it,
the third to diſepiſe counſell.

461. The greateſt ſtep is that out of
doores.

462. To weepe for joy is a kinde of
Manna.

463. The firſt ſervice a child doth his
father is to make him fooliſh.

464. The reſolved minde hath no
cares.

465. In the kingdome of a cheater, the
wallet is carried before.

466. The eye will have his part.

467. The good mother ſayes not, will
you? but gives.

468. A houſe and a woman ſute excel-
lently.

469. In the kingdome of blindmen the
one ey'd is king,

470. A

✤✤✤✤✤✤✤✤✤✤✤✤✤✤✤✤✤✤✤✤✤✤✤

470. A little Kitchin makes a large house.

471. Warre makes theeves, and peace hangs them.

472. Poverty is the mother of health.

473. In the morning mountaines, in the evening fountaines.

474. The back-doore robs the house.

475. Wealth is like rheume, it falles on the weakest parts.

476. The gowne is his that weares it, and the world his that enjoyes it.

477. Hope is the poore mans bread.

478. Vertue now is in herbs and stones and words onely.

479. Fine words dresse ill deedes.

480. Labour as long liu'd, pray as even dying.

481. A poore beauty finds more lovers then husbands.

482. Discreet women have neither eyes nor eares.

483. Things well fitted abide.

484. Prettinesse dies first.

485. Talking payes no toll.

486. The masters eye fattens the horse, and his foote the ground.

C 2   487. Dif-

❖❖❖❖❖❖❖❖❖❖❖❖❖❖❖❖❖❖❖❖❖

487. Disgraces are like cherries, one drawes another.

488. Praise a hill, but keepe below.

489. Praise the Sea, but keepe on land.

490. In chusing a wife, and buying a sword, we ought not to trust another.

491. The wearer knowes, where the shoe wrings.

492. Faire is not faire, but that which pleaseth.

493. There is no jollitie but hath a smack of folly.

494. He that's long agiving, knowes not how to give.

495. The filth under the white snow, the sunne discovers.

496. Every one fastens where there is gaine.

497. All feete tread not in one shoe.

498. Patience, time and money accommodate all things.

499. For want of a naile the shoe is lost, for want of a shoe the horse is lost, for want of a horse the rider is lost.

500. Weigh justly and sell dearely.

501. Little wealth little care.

502. Little journeys and good cost, bring

bring safe home.

　503. Gluttony kills more then the sword.

　504. When children stand quiet, they have done some ill.

　505. A little and good fills the trencher.

　506. A penny spar'd is twice got.

　507. When a knave is in a plumtree he hath neither friend nor kin.

　508. Short boughs, long vintage.

　509. Health without money, is halfe an ague.

　510. If the wise erred not, it would goe hard with fooles.

　511. Beare with evill, and expect good.

　512. He that tells a secret, is anothers servant.

　513. If all fooles wore white Caps, wee should seeme a flock of geese.

　514. Water, fire, and souldiers, quickly make roome.

　515. Pension never inriched young man.

　516. Vnder water, famine, under snow bread.

　517. The Lame goes as farre as your staggerer.　　C 3　　518. He

✢✢✢✢✢✢✢✢✢✢✢✢✢✢✢✢✢✢✢✢✢✢✢

518. He that looſeth is Marchant as well as he that gaines.

519. A jade eates as much as a good horſe.

520. All things in their beeing are good for ſomething.

521. One flower makes no garland.

522. A faire death honours the whole life.

523. One enemy is too much.

524. Living well is the beſt revenge.

525. One foole makes a hundred.

526. One paire of eares drawes dry a hundred tongues.

527. A foole may throw a ſtone into a well, which a hundred wiſe men cannot pull out.

528. One ſlumber finds another.

529. On a good bargaine thinke twice.

530. To a good ſpender God is the Treaſurer.

531. A curſt Cow hath ſhott hornes.

532. Muſick helps not the tooth-ach.

533. We cannot come to honour under Coverlet.

534. Great paines quickly find eaſe.

535. To the counſell of fooles a wood-den bell.

536. The

536. The cholerick man never wants woe.

537. Helpe thy selfe, and God will helpe thee.

538. At the games end we shall see who gaines.

539. There are many waies to fame.

540. Love is the true price of love.

541. Love rules his kingdome without a sword.

542. Love makes all hard hearts gentle.

543. Love makes a good eye squint.

544. Love askes faith, and faith firmenesse.

545. A scepter is one thing, and a ladle another.

546. Great trees are good for nothing but shade.

547. Hee commands enough that obeyes a wise man.

548. Faire words makes mee looke to my purse.

549. Though the Fox run, the chicken hath wings.

750. He plaies well that winnes.

551. You must strike in measure, when

C 4   there

✤✤✤✤✤✤✤✤✤✤ ✤✤ ✤✤✤✤✤✤✤✤✤✤✤✤✤

there are many to ftrike on one Anvile.

551. The fhorteft anfwer is doing.

553. It's a poore ftake that cannot ftand one yeare in the ground.

554. He that commits a fault, thinkes every one fpeakes of it.

555. He that's foolifh in the fault, let him be wife in the punifhment.

556. The blind eate many a flie.

557. He that can make a fire well, can end a quarrell.

558. The tooth-ach is more eafe, then to deale with ill people.

559. Hee that fhould have what hee hath not, fhould doe what he doth not.

560. He that hath no good trade, it is to his loffe.

561. The offender never pardons.

562. He that lives not well one yeare, forrowes feven after.

563. He that hopes not for good, feares not evill.

564. He that is angry at a feaft is rude.

565. He that mockes a cripple, ought to be whole.

566. When the tree is fallen, all goe with their hatchet.

567. He

❧❧❧❧❧❧❧❧❧❧❧❧❧❧❧❧❧❧❧

567. He that hath hornes in his bosom,
let him not put them on his head.

568. He that burnes most shines most.

569. He that trusts in a lie, shall perish
in truth.

570. Hee that blowes in the dust fills
his eyes with it.

571. Bells call others, but themselves
enter not into the Church.

572. Of faire things, the Autumne is
faire.

573. Giving is dead, restoring very
sicke.

574. A gift much expected is paid, not
given.

575. Two ill meales make the third a
glutton.

576. The Royall Crowne cures not
the head-ach.

577. 'Tis hard to be wretched, but worse
to be knowne so.

578. A feather in hand is better then a
bird in the ayre.

579. It's better to be head of a Lyzard,
then the tayle of a Lyon.

580 Good & quickly seldome meete.

581. Folly growes without watering.

582. Hap-

✢✢✢✢✢✢✢✢✢✢✢✢✢✢✢✢✢✢✢✢✢✢

582. Happier are the hands compast with yron, then a heart with thoughts.

583 If the staffe be crooked, the shaddow cannot be straight.

584. To take the nuts from the fire with the dogges foot.

585. He is a foole that makes a wedge of his fist.

586. Valour that parlies, is neare yeelding.

587. Thursday come, and the week's gone.

588. A flatterers throat is an open Sepulcher.

589. There is great force hidden in a sweet command.

590. The command of custome is great.

591. To have money is a feare, not to have it a griefe.

592. The Catt sees not the mouse ever.

593. Little dogs start the Hare, the great get her.

594. Willowes are weake, yet they bind other wood.

595. A good prayer is master of anothers purse.   596. The

✦✦✦✦✦✦✦✦✦✦✦✦✦✦✦✦✦✦✦✦

596. The thread breakes, where it is weakeſt.

597. Old men, when they ſcorne young make much of death.

598. God is at the end, when we thinke he is furtheſt off it.

599. A good Judge conceives quickly, judges ſlowly.

600. Rivers neede a ſpring.

601. He that contemplates, hath a day without night.

602. Give looſers leave to talke.

603. Loſſe embraceth ſhame.

604. Gaming, women, and wine, while they laugh they make men pine.

605. The fatt man knoweth not, what the leane thinketh.

606. Wood halfe burnt is eaſily kindled.

607. The fiſh adores the bait.

608. He that goeth farre hath many encounters.

609. Every bees hony is ſweet.

610. The ſlothfull is the ſervant of the counters.

611. Wiſedome hath one foot on Land, and another on Sea.

612. The

✦✦✦✦✦✦✦✦✦✦✦ ✦✦✦✦✦✦✦✦✦✦✦✦

612. The thought hath good leggs, and the quill a good tongue.

613. A wise man needes not blush for changing his purpose.

614. The March sunne raises but dissolves not.

615 Time is the Rider that breakes youth.

616. The wine in the bottell doth not quench thirst.

617. The sight of a man hath the force of a Lyon.

618. An examin'd enterprize, goes on boldly.

619. In every Art it is good to have a master.

620. In every country dogges bite.

621. In every countrey the sun rises in the morning.

622. A noble plant suites not with a stubborne ground.

623. You may bring a horse to the river, but he will drinke when and what he pleaseth.

624. Before you make a friend, eate a bushell of salt with him.

625. Speake fitly, or be silent wisely.

626. Skill

626. Skill and confidence are an unconquered army.

627. I was taken by a morsell, saies the fish.

628. A disarmed peace is weake.

629. The ballance distinguisheth not betweene gold and lead.

630. The perswasion of the fortunate swaies the doubtfull.

631. To bee beloved is above all bargaines.

632. To deceive ones selfe is very easie.

633. The reasons of the poore weigh not.

634. Perversnes makes one squint ey'd.

635. The evening praises the day, and the morning a frost.

636. The table robbes more then a thiefe.

637. When age is jocond it makes sport for death.

638. True praise rootes and spreedes.

639. Feares are divided in the midst.

640. The soule needes few things, the body many.

641. Astrologie is true, but the Astrologers cannot finde it.　　642. Ty

✦✦✦✦✦✦✦✦✦✦✦✦✦✦✦✦✦✦✦✦✦✦✦✦

642. Ty it well, and let it goe.

643. Emptic veſſels found moſt.

644. Send not a Catt for Lard.

645. Fooliſh tongues talke by the dozen.

646. Love makes one fitt for any work.

647. A pittifull mother makes a ſcald head.

648. An old Phyſitian, and a young Lawyer.

649. Talke much and erre much, ſaies the Spanyard.

650. Some make a conſcience of ſpitting in the Church, yet robbe the Altar.

651. An idle head is a boxe for the winde.

652. Shew me a lyer, and ile ſhew thee a theefe.

653. A beane in liberty, is better then a comfit in priſon.

654. None is borne Maſter.

655. Shew a good man his errour and he turnes it to a vertue, but an ill, it doubles his fault.

656. None is offended but by himſelfe.

657. None ſaies his Garner is full.

658. In

658. In the husband, wisedome, in the wife gentlenesse.

659. Nothing dries sooner then a teare.

660. In a Leopard the spotts are not observed.

661. Nothing lasts but the Church.

662. A wise man cares not for what he cannot have.

663. It's not good fishing before the net.

664. He cannot be vertuous that is not rigorous.

665. That which will not be spun, let it not come betweene the spindle and the distaffe.

666. When my house burnes, it's not good playing at Chesse.

667. No barber shaves so close, but another finds worke.

668. Ther's no great banquet, but some fares ill.

669. A holy habit clenseth not a foule soule.

670. Forbeare not sowing, because of birds.

671. Mention not a halter in the house of him that was hanged.

672. Speake

✦✦✦✦✦✦✦✦✦✦✦✦✦✦ ✦✦✦✦✦✦✦✦✦✦✦✦

672. Speake not of a dead man at the table.

673. A hatt is not made for one showr.

674. No sooner is a Temple built to God but the Devill builds a Chappell hard by.

675. Every one puts his fault on the Times.

676. You cannot make a wind-mill goe with a paire of bellowes.

677. Pardon all but thy selfe.

678. Every one is weary, the poore in seeking, the rich in keeping, the good in learning.

679. The escaped mouse ever feeles the taste of the bait.

680. A litle wind kindles; much puts out the fire.

681. Dry bread at home is better then roft meate abroad.

682. More have repented speech then silence.

683. The coveteous spends more then the liberall.

684. Divine ashes are better then earthly meale.

685. Beauty drawes more then oxen.

686. One father is more then a hundred Schoolemasters.   687. One

687. One eye of the masters sees more, then ten of the servants.

688. When God will punish, hee will first take away the understanding.

689. A little labour, much health.

690. When it thunders, the theefe becomes honest.

691. The tree that God plants, no winde hurts it.

692. Knowledge is no burthen.

693. It's a bold mouse that nestles in the catts eare.

694. Long jesting was never good.

695. If a good man thrive, all thrive with him.

696. If the mother had not beene in the oven, shee had never sought her daughter there.

697 If great men would have care of little ones, both would last long.

698. Though you see a Church-man ill, yet continue in the Church still.

699. Old praise dies, unlesse you feede it.

700. If things were to be done twice, all would be wise.

701. Had you the world on your

D

Chesse-bord, you could not fit all to your mind.

702. Suffer and expect.

703. If fooles should not foole it, they should loose their seafon.

704. Love and businesse teach eloquence.

705. That which two will, takes effect.

706. He complaines wrongfully on the sea that twice suffers shipwrack.

707. He is onely bright that shines by himselfe.

708. A valiant mans looke is more then a cowards sword.

709. The effect speakes, the tongue needes not.

710. Divine grace was never slow.

711. Reason lies betweene the spurre and the bridle.

712. It's a proud horse that will not carry his owne provender.

713. Three women make a market.

714. Three can hold their peace, if two be away.

715. It's an ill councell that hath no scape.

716. All

✠✠✠✠✠✠✠✠✠✠✠✠✠✠✠✠✠✠✠✠✠

716. All our pompe the earth covers.

717. To whirle the eyes too much shewes a Kites braine.

718. Comparitons are odious.

719. All keyes hang not on one girdle.

720 Great businesses turne on a little pinne.

721. The wind in ones face makes one wise.

722. All the Armes of England will not arme feare.

723. One sword keepes another in the sheath.

724. Be what thou wouldst seeme to be.

725. Let all live as they would die.

726. A gentle heart is tyed with an easie thread.

727 Sweet discourse makes short daies and nights.

728. God provides for him that trusteth.

729. He that will not have peace, God gives him warre.

730. To him that will, waies are not wanting.

✤✤✤✤✤✤✤✤✤✤✤✤✤✤✤✤✤✤✤✤✤✤

731. To a great night a great Lanthorne.

732. To a child all weather is cold.

733. Where there is peace, God is.

734. None is so wise, but the foole overtakes him.

735. Fooles give, to pleafe all, but their owne.

736. Profperity lets goe the bridle.

737. The Frier preached againft ftealing, and had a goofe in his fleeve.

738. To be too bufie gets contempt.

739. February makes a bridge and March breakes it.

740. A horfe ftumbles that hath foure legges.

741. The beft fmell is bread, the beft favour, falt, the beft love that of children.

742. That's the beft gowne that goes up and downe the houfe.

743. The market is the beft garden.

744. The firft difh pleafeth all.

745. The higher the Ape goes, the more he fhewes his taile.

746. Night is the mother of Councels.

747. Gods Mill grinds flow, but fure.

748. Every

❧❧❧❧❧❧❧❧❧❧❧❧❧❧❧❧❧❧❧❧❧❧

748. Every one thinkes his sacke heaviest.

749. Drought never brought dearth.

750. All complaine.

751. Gamsters and race-horses never last long..

752. It's a poore sport that's not worth the candle.

753. He that is fallen cannot helpe him that is downe.

754. Every one is witty for his owne purpose.

755. A little lett lets an ill workeman.

756. Good workemen are seldome rich.

757. By doing nothing we learne to do ill.

758. A great dowry is a bed full of brables.

759. No profit to honour, no honour to Religion.

760. Every sin brings it's punishment with it.

761. Of him that speakes ill, consider the life more then the words.

762. You cannot hide an eele in a sacke.

763. Give not S. *Peter* so much, to leave

Saint

✠✠✠✠✠✠✠✠✠✠✠✠✠✠✠✠✠✠✠✠✠✠✠✠

Saint *Paul* nothing.

764. You cannot flea a ftone.

765. The chiefe difeafe that raignes this yeare is folly.

766. A fleepy mafter makes his fervant a Lowt.

767. Better fpeake truth rudely, then lye covertly.

768. He that feares leaves, let him not goe into the wood.

769 One foote is better then two crutches.

770. Better fuffer ill, then doe ill.

771. Neither praife nor difpraife thy felfe, thy actions ferve the turne.

772. Soft and faire goes farre.

773. The conftancy of the benefit of the yeere in their feafons, argues a Deity.

774. Praife none to much, for all are fickle.

775. It's abfurd to warme one in his armour.

776. Law futes confume time, and mony, and reft, and friends.

777. Nature drawes more then ten reemes.

778. Hee that hath a wife and children wants not bufineffe.

779, A

✠✠✠✠✠✠✠✠✠✠✠✠✠✠✠✠✠✠✠✠

780. A shippe and a woman are ever repairing.

781. He that feares death lives not.

782. He that pitties another, remembers himselfe.

783. He that doth what he should not, shall feele what he would not.

784. Hee that marries for wealth sells his liberty.

785. He that once hitts, is ever bending.

786. He that serves, must serve.

787. He that lends, gives.

788. He that preacheth giveth almes.

789. He that cockers his child, provides for his enemie.

790. A pittifull looke askes enough.

791. Who will sell the Cow, must say the word.

792. Service is no Inheritance.

793. The faulty stands on his guard.

794. A kinsman, a friend, or whom you intreate, take not to serve you, if you will be served neately.

795. At Court, every one for himselfe.

796. To a crafty man, a crafty and an halfe.

797. Hee that is throwne, would ever wrestle.　　D 4　　798. He

❀❀❀❀❀❀❀❀❀❀❀❀❀❀❀❀❀❀❀❀❀❀❀❀

798. He that ferves well needes not ask his wages.

799 Faire language grates not the tongue.

800. A good heart cannot lye.

801. Good fwimmers at length are drowned.

802 Good land, evill way.

803. In doing we learne.

804. It's good walking with a horfe in ones hand.

805. God, and Parents, and our Mafter, can never be requited.

806. An ill deede cannot bring honour,

807. A fmall heart hath fmall defires.

808. All are not merry that dance lightly.

809. Curtefie on one fide only lafts not long.

810. Wine-Counfels feldome profper.

811. Weening is not meafure.

812. The beft of the fport is to doe the deede, and fay nothing.

813. If thou thy felfe canft doe it, attend no others helpe or hand.

814. Of a little thing a little difpleafeth.

815. He

815 He warmes too neere that burnes.

816. God keepe me from foure houses,
an Vsurers, a Taverne, a Spittle, and a Pri-
son.

817. In hundred elles of contention,
there is not an inch of love.

818. Doe what thou oughtest, and come
what come can.

819. Hunger makes dinners, pastime
suppers.

820. In a long journey straw waighs.

821. Women laugh when they can,
and weepe when they will.

822. Warre is deaths feast.

823. Set good against evill.

824. Hee that brings good newes
knockes hard.

825. Beate the dog before the Lyon.

826. Hast comes not alone.

827. You must loose a flie to catch a
trout.

828. Better a snotty child, then his nose
wip'd off.

829. No prison is faire, nor love foule.

830. Hee is not free that drawes his
chaine.

831. Hee goes not out of his way, that
goes to a good Inne.   832. There

✤✤✤✤✤✤✤✤✤✤✤✤✤✤✤✤✤✤✤✤✤✤

833. There come nought out of the ſacke but what was there.

834. A little given ſeaſonably, excuſes a great gift.

835. Hee lookes not well to himſelfe that lookes not ever.

836. He thinkes not well, that thinkes not againe.

837. Religion, Credit, and the Eye are not to be touched.

838. The tongue is not ſteele, yet it cuts.

839. A white wall is the paper of a foole.

840. They talke of Chriſtmas ſo long, that it comes.

841. That is gold which is worth gold.

842. It's good tying the ſack before it be full.

843. Words are women, deedes are men.

844. Poverty is no ſinne.

845. A ſtone in a well is not loſt.

846. He can give little to his ſervant, that lickes his knife.

847. Promiſing is the eve of giving.

848. Hee that keepes his owne makes warre.   849. The

✿✿✿✿✿✿✿✿✿✿✿✿✿✿✿✿✿✿✿✿✿

849. The Wolfe must dye in his owne skinne.

850. Goods are theirs that enjoy them.

851. He that sends a foole expects one.

852. He that can stay obtaines.

853. Hee that gaines well and spends well, needes no count booke.

854. He that endures, is not overcome.

855. He that gives all, before hee dies provides to suffer.

856. He that talkes much of his happinesse summons griefe.

857. Hee that loves the tree, loves the branch

858. Who hastens a glutton choakes him.

859. Who praiseth Saint *Peter*, doth not blame Saint *Paul*.

860. He that hath not the craft, let him shut up shop.

861. He that knowes nothing, doubts nothing.

862. Greene wood makes a hott fire.

863. He that marries late, marries ill.

864. He that passeth a winters day escapes an enemy.

865. The Rich knowes not who is his friend.

866. A

866. A morning sunne, and a wine-bred child, and a latin-bred woman, seldome end well.

867. To a close shorne sheepe, God gives wind by measure.

868 A pleasure long expected, is deare enough sold.

869. A poore mans Cow dies rich mans child.

870. The Cow knowes not what her taile is worth, till she have lost it.

871. Chuse a horse made, and a wife to make.

872. It's an ill aire where wee gaine nothing.

873. Hee hath not liv'd, that lives not after death.

874. So many men in Court and so many strangers.

875. He quits his place well, that leaves his friend there.

876. That which sufficeth is not little.

877. Good newes may bee told at any time, but ill in the morning.

878. Hee that would be a Gentleman, let him goe to an assault.

879. Who paies the Physitian, does the cure.   880. None

880. None knowes the weight of anothers burthen.

881. Every one hath a foole in his sleeve.

882. One houres sleepe before midnight, is worth three after.

883. In a retreat the lame are formost.

884. It's more paine to doe nothing then something.

885. Amongst good men two men suffice.

886. There needs a long time to know the worlds pulse.

887. The ofspring of those that are very young, or very old, lasts not.

888. A Tyrant is most tyrant to himselfe.

889. Too much taking heede is losse.

890. Craft against craft, makes no living.

891. The Reverend are ever before.

892. *France* is a meddow that cuts thrice a yeere.

893. 'Tis easier to build two chimneys, then to maintaine one.

894. The Court hath no Almanack.

895. He that will enter into Paradise, must

✣✤✣✤✣✤✣✤✣✤✣✤✣✤✣✤✣✤✣✤✣✤✣

muſt have a good key.

896. When you enter into a houſe, leave the anger ever at the doore.

897. Hee hath no leiſure who uſeth it not.

898. It's a wicked thing to make a dearth ones garner.

899. He that deales in the world needes foure ſeeves.

900. Take heede of an oxe before, of an horſe behind, of a monke on all ſides.

901. The yeare doth nothing elſe but open and ſhut.

902. The ignorant hath an Eagles wings, and an Owles eyes.

903. There are more Phyſitians in health then drunkards.

904. The wife is the key of the houſe.

905. The Law is not the ſame at morning and at night.

906. Warre and Phyſicke are governed by the eye.

907. Halfe the world knowes not how the other halfe lies.

908. Death keepes no Calender.

909. Ships feare fire more then water.

910. The leaſt fooliſh is wiſe.

911. The

911. The chiefe boxe of health is time.

912. Silkes and Satins put out the fire in the chimney.

913. The first blow is as much as two.

914 The life of man is a winter way.

915. The way is an ill neighbour.

916. An old mans staffe is the rapper of deaths doore.

917. Life is halfe spent before we know, what it is.

918. The singing man keepes his shop in his throate.

919. The body is more drest then the soule.

920. The body is sooner drest then the soule.

921. The Physitian owes all to the patient, but the patient owes nothing to him but a little mony.

922. The little cannot bee great, unlesse he devoure many.

923. Time undermines us.

924. The Chollerick drinkes, the Melancholick eates; the Flegmatick sleepes.

925. The Apothecaries morter spoiles the Luters musick.

926. Conversation makes one what he is.

✠✠✠✠✠✠✠✠✠✠✠✠✠✠✠✠✠✠✠✠✠✠

927. The deafe gaines the injury.

928. Yeeres know more then bookes.

929. Wine is a turne-coate (firſt a friend, then an enemy.)

930. Wine ever paies for his lodging.

931. Wine makes all ſorts of creatures at table.

932. Wine that coſt nothing is digeſted before it be drunke.

933. Trees eate but once.

934. Armour is light at table.

935. Good horſes make ſhort miles.

936. Caſtles are Forreſts of ſtones.

937. The dainties of the great, are the teares of the poore.

938. Parſons are ſoules waggoners.

939. Children when they are little make parents fooles, when they are great they make them mad.

940. The M. abſent, and the houſe dead.

941. Dogs are fine in the field.

942. Sinnes are not knowne till they bee acted.

943. Thornes whiten yet doe nothing.

944. All are preſumed good, till they are found in a fault.

945. The great put the little on the hooke.   946. The

✚✚✚✚✚✚✚✚✚✚✚✚✚✚✚✚✚✚✚✚✚

946. The great would have none great and the little all little.

947 The Italians are wise before the deede, the Germanes in the deede, the French after the deede.

949. Every mile is two in winter.

950. Spectacles are deaths Harquebuze.

951. Lawyers houses are built on the heads of fooles.

952. The house is a fine house, when good folke are within.

953. The best bred have the best portion.

954. The first and last frosts are the worst.

955. Gifts enter every where without a wimble.

956. Princes have no way.

957. Knowledge makes one laugh, but wealth makes one dance.

958. The Citizen is at his businesse before he rise.

959. The eyes have one language every where.

960. It is better to have wings then hornes.

961. Better be a foole then a knave.

H   962. Count

✦✦✦✦✦✦✦✦✦✦✦✦✦✦✦✦✦✦✦✦✦

962. Count not fowre except you have them in a wallett.

963. To live peaceably with all breedes good blood.

964. You may be on land, yet not in a garden.

965. You cannot make the fire so low but it will get out.

966. Wee know not who lives or dies?

967. An Oxe is taken by the horns, and a Man by the tongue.

968. Manie things are lost for want of asking.

969. No Church-yard is so handsom, that a man would desire straight to bee buried there.

970. Citties are taken by the eares.

971. Once a yeare a man may say: on his confidence.

972. Wee leave more to do when wee dye, then wee have done.

973. With customes wee live well, but Lawes undoe us.

674. To speake of an Vsurer at the table, marres the wine.

975. Paines to get, care to keep, feare to lose.

976. For

976. For a morning raine leave not your journey.

277. One faire day in winter makes not birds merrie.

278 Hee that learnes a trade hath a purchase made.

279. When all men have, what belongs to them, it cannot bee much.

980. Though God take the sunne out of the Heaven yet we must have patience.

981. When a man sleepes, his head is in his stomach.

982. When one is on horsebacke hee knowes all things.

983. When God is made master of a family, he orders the disorderly.

984. When a Lackey comes to hells doore the devills locke the gates.

985. He that is at ease, seekes dainties.

986. Hee that hath charge of soules, transports them not in bundles.

987. Hee that tells his wife newes is but newly married.

988. Hee that is in a towne in May, loseth his spring.

989. Hee that is in a Taverne, thinkes he is in a vine-garden.

D 2 990. He

✦✦✦✦✦✦✦✦✦✦✦✦✦✦✦✦✦✦✦✦✦✦✦✦

990. He that praiſeth himſelfe, ſpatte-
reth himſelfe.

991. Hee that is a maſter muſt ſerve
(another.)

992. He that is ſurprized with the firſt
froſt, feeles it all the winter after.

993. Hee a beaſt doth die, that hath
done no good to his countſy.

994. He that followes the Lord hopes
to goe before.

995. He that dies without the compa-
ny of good men, puts not himſelfe into a
good way.

996. Who hath no head, needes no
hatt.

997. Who hath no haſt in his buſineſſe,
mountaines to him ſeeme valleys.

998. Speake not of my debts, unleſſe
you meane to pay them.

999. He that is not in the warres is not
out of danger.

1000. He that gives me ſmall gifts,
would have me live.

1001. He that is his owne Counſellor,
knowes nothing ſure but what hee hath
laid out.

1002. He that hath lands hath quarrells.

103. He

1003. Hee that goes to bed thirsty, ri-
seth healthy.

1004. Who will make a doore of gold
must knock a naile every day.

1005. A trade is better then service.

1006 Hee that lives in hope danceth
without musick.

1007. To review ones store is to mow
twice.

1008. Saint *Luke* was a Saint and a
Physitian, yet is dead.

1009. Without businesse debauchery.

1010. Without danger we cannot get
beyond danger.

1011. Health and sicknesse surely are
mens double enemies.

1012. If gold knew what gold is, gold
would get gold I wis.

1013. Little losses amaze, great, tame.

1014. Chuse none for thy servant, who
have served thy betters.

1015. Service without reward is pu-
nishment.

1016. If the husband be not at home,
there is nobodie.

1017. An oath that is not to bee made,
is not to be kept.

1018. The

1018. The eye is bigger then the belly.

1019. If you would bee at ease, all the world is not.

1020. Were it not for the bone in the legge, all the world would turne Carpenters (to make them crutches.)

1021. If you must flie, flie well.

1022. All that shakes falles not.

1023. All beasts of prey, are strong or treacherous.

1024. If the braine sowes not corne, it plants thistles.

1025. A man well mounted, is ever Cholerick.

1026. Every one is a master and servant.

1027. A piece of a Churchyard fits every body.

1028. One month doth nothing without another.

1029. A master of straw eates a servant of steele.

1030. An old cat sports not with her prey

1031. A woman conceales what shee knowes not.

1032. Hee that wipes the childs nose, kisseth the mothers cheeke.

FINIS.

Index of Authors

Brathwait, Richard (1588–1673)
educ. Oriel College, Oxford (*matric.* 1605); Pembroke College, Cambridge; Gray's Inn; J.P. for Westmoreland. Poet
314, E21, E98, E101

Browne, William (1590?–1645?)
educ. Tavistock grammar school; Exeter College, Oxford, *c.* 1603 (*matric.* 1624, M.A. 1625); Inner Temple, from Clifford's Inn, 1611; later attached to household of Herbert family, Earls of Pembroke. Poet
E38, E44

Burghe, Nicholas (*d.*1670)
Royalist captain in Civil War
E56, E116

Carew, Thomas (1594/5–1640)
educ. Merton College, Oxford (*matric.* 1608, B.A. 1611); Middle Temple, 1612; diplomatic appointments in Italy, the Hague and Paris, 1613–19; Gentleman of the Privy Chamber, 1628, and subsequently Sewer in Ordinary to the King
124, 179, 268, 274, 462, E49

Clavell, John (1601–43)
educ. Brasenose College, Oxford (*matric.* 1619). Dramatist and highwayman
473

Corbett, Richard (1582–1635)
educ. Westminster School; Broadgates Hall [Pembroke College], Oxford (*matric.* 1598); Christ Church, Oxford, 1599 (B.A. 1602, M.A. 1605, D.D. 1617); Proctor, 1612; Dean of Christ Church, 1620; Bishop of Oxford, 1628–32; Bishop of Norwich, 1632–5
469, E44, E57

Marlowe, Christopher (1564–93)
educ. King's School, Canterbury; Corpus Christi College, Cambridge (*matric.* 1580–1, B.A. 1583–4, M.A. 1587). Dramatist and poet

169, 217

Martyn, Joseph (*fl.*1621)
Epigrammatist

4, 297, 432, 435

May, Edward (*fl.*1633)
Epigrammatist; possibly divine, chaplain to Lincoln's Inn
387, 392–6, 502

May, Thomas (1595–1650)
educ. Sidney Sussex College, Cambridge (*matric.* 1609, B.A. 1612–13); Gray's Inn, 1615; Secretary for Parliament, 1646–50. Author, dramatist

292*, 294*, 328*

Milton, John (1608–74)
educ. St Paul's School; Christ's College, Cambridge (*matric.* 1625, B.A. 1629, M.A. 1632); schoolmaster, polemical author; Latin secretary to the Council of State, 1649–60. Poet

E96

Molle, Henry (*c.*1597–1658)
educ. Eton College; King's College, Cambridge (*matric.* 1612, B.A. 1616–17, M.A. 1620, Fellow 1615–50, 1654–8); Vice-Provost; Senior Proctor, 1633–4; Public Orator, 1639–50

172

Morley, George (1598–1684)
educ. Westminster School; Christ Church, Oxford, 1615 (B.A. 1618, M.A. 1621, D.D. 1642); member of Great Tew circle; Canon of Christ Church, 1641; Royal Chaplain; Dean of Christ Church, 1660; Bishop of Worcester, 1660–2; Bishop of Winchester, 1662–84

E75

Stone, Benjamin (*b. c.*1585)
   educ. New College, Oxford (*matric.* 1605, B.A. 1609)
                                                              E42

Strode, William (1602–45)
   educ. Westminster School; Christ Church, Oxford, 1617
   (*matric.* 1621, B.A. 1621, M.A. 1624, B.D. 1631, D.D.
   1638); chaplain to Richard Corbett, 1628; Public Orator of
   Oxford University, 1629–45; Canon (1638) and Sub-Dean
   of Christ Church, 1639–43. Poet and dramatist
                                     165, 180, 209, 215, E38

Taylor, John (1580–1653)
   educ. Gloucester Grammar School; Oriel College, Oxford
   (*matric.* 1606, B.A. 1609, M.A. 1614, B.D. 1629). Divine
                                                         226, 487

Tompson, J.
                                                              461

Turner, Richard (*fl.*1522–52)
   educ. Magdalen College, Oxford (B.A. 1531, M.A. 1535,
   B.D. 1536, D.D. 1551–2); Canon of Windsor, 1551. Divine
                                                              457

W., F.
                                                             178*

Weever, John (1576–1632)
   educ. Queen's College, Cambridge, 1594 (B.A. 1597–8).
   Poet and antiquary
                                            311, 381–3, 496

Wotton, Sir Henry (1568–1639)
   educ. Winchester School; New College, Oxford (*matric.*
   1584); Queen's College, Oxford (B.A. 1588); Middle
   Temple, 1595; Provost of Eton College, 1624–39.
   Diplomatist
                                                         472, E40

Index of Titles

Index of First Lines